10/2010

DUCKS & GEESE

of MINNESOTA FIELD GUIDE

Includes Swans & Other Water Birds

by Stan Tekiela

Adventure Publications, Inc.
Cambridge, Minnesota

To my wife Katherine and daughter Abigail with all my love

Acknowledgments

Special thanks to the National Wildlife Refuge System along with state and local agencies, both public and private, for stewarding lands that are critical to the many bird species we so love.

Edited by Sandy Livoti
Cover and book design by Jonathan Norberg
Illustrations by Julie Martinez
Range maps by Anthony Hertzel

Photo credits by photographer and page number:
Cover photos: Canada Goose, Mallard and Common Loon by Stan Tekiela
Rick and Nora Bowers: 50 (both), 52 (both), 76 (inset), 92 (insets 1-2), 96 (inset 3), 106 (male), 120 (inset 4), 124 (inset 2), 136 (inset 3), 152 (pattern, insets 2-3), 160 (inset 2), 164 (top, inset 1), 192 (inset 2), 198, 222 (bottom), 224 (top), 228 (top, inset 3), 232 (inset 2) **Sharon Cummings/DPA***: 38 (inset 2) **Larry Ditto/KAC***: 80 (inset 3) **Don Enger**: 208 (insets 1-2) **Kevin T. Karlson**: 76 (inset 3), 104 (top, inset 4), 106 (female), 108 (inset 1), 128 (pattern), 144 (both), 164 (pattern), 220 (inset 3), 228 (pattern, inset 2), 240 (top) **Maslowski Productions**: 48 (top), 76 (top, pattern, inset 1), 80 (top, inset 1), 104 (inset 1), 146 (both), 148, 200 (top), 252 (inset 2) **Neil Mishler/Windigo***: 124 (top) **John Pennoyer**: 116 (pattern) **Jeffrey Rich/KAC***: 240 (inset 1) **Jim Roetzel/DPA***: 238 **Brian E. Small**: 122 (male), 130 (both), 138 (male), 142 (female), 244 (inset 2) **Stan Tekiela**: 32 (both), 34 (all), 36 (both), 38 (top, insets 1, 3-4), 40 (both), 42 (all), 44 (both), 46 (both), 48 (pattern, insets 1-3), 54 (both), 56 (all), 58, 60 (inset 1), 62, 64 (all), 66 (both), 68 (all), 70 (both), 72 (all), 74 (both), 78 (both), 80 (inset 2), 82 (both), 84 (all), 86 (all), 88 (all), 90 (both), 92 (inset 3), 94 (both), 96 (top, insets 1-2, 4), 98 (both), 100 (all), 102 (male), 104 (insets 2-3), 110 (both), 112 (top, insets 1-3), 114 (both), 116 (top, insets 1-3), 118 (both), 120 (top, insets 1-3), 122 (female), 124 (pattern, inset 1), 126 (both), 134 (both), 140 (inset 1), 142 (male), 150, 152 (top, inset 1), 154, 156 (all), 162, 166, 168 (all), 170, 172 (all), 174 (both), 176 (both), 178, 180 (all), 182 (both), 184 (both), 186, 188 (all), 190, 192 (top, inset 1), 194, 196 (all), 200 (inset 1), 202, 204, 206, 208 (top), 210, 212, 214, 216 (all), 218, 220 (top, insets 1-2), 222 (top), 224 (insets 1-4), 226 (both), 228 (inset 1), 230 (both), 232 (top, insets 1, 3), 234, 242, 244 (top, insets 1, 3), 246, 248 (all), 250, 252 (top, pattern, insets 1, 3) **Tom Vezo**: 108 (top), 236 (inset 1) **Jim Zipp**: 92 (top), 112 (pattern), 128 (top, insets 1-3), 132 (all), 136 (top, pattern, insets 1-2, 4), 138 (female), 140 (top, pattern), 158, 160 (top, pattern, insets 1, 3-4), 236 (top)
*DPA: Dembinsky Photo Associates; KAC: KAC Productions; Windigo: Windigo Images
To the best of the publisher's knowledge, all photos were of live birds.

Published by Adventure Publications, Inc.
820 Cleveland St. S
Cambridge, MN 55008
1-800-678-7006
www.adventurepublications.net
Printed in China
ISBN-13: 978-1-59193-133-1
ISBN-10: 1-59193-133-9

TABLE OF CONTENTS

Introduction

Waterfowl

Dabbling Ducks

Other Water Birds

Index

About the Author

DUCKS AND GEESE OF MINNESOTA

Ducks and geese are spectacular and diverse birds that make up a larger group of birds known as waterfowl. Waterfowl includes some of the most beautifully colored birds, such as the male Wood Duck and Cinnamon Teal, and some of the largest members of the bird world—the swans.

The scientific classification of waterfowl places ducks, geese and swans in one family called *Anatidae*. This is a very large, complex group of birds with many waterfowl species—around 154 worldwide. Waterfowl are found on all continents and on many isolated islands. Just about anywhere you go—from the frozen Arctic to the tropical rain forests to the ice-covered Antarctic regions—you can find some kind of waterfowl. The good news is you don't have to go very far to find many of them right here in Minnesota!

We have 50 species of native waterfowl in North America and an additional dozen or more non-native birds. Of these, 46 occur in Minnesota, 8 of which are not native. Non-native birds have been introduced into the wild for a variety of reasons and, while those species are not common in Minnesota, they can be seen with some regularity in certain areas. This field guide includes 59 species—all 46 native and non-native waterfowl species along with 13 other water birds that look or act like ducks, geese or swans, but actually are not waterfowl.

IS IT A WATERFOWL OR OTHER WATER BIRD?

We have many terms for the birds we see on water, but we use them generally and loosely. These terms are not synonomous with waterfowl. Some people use the general term "ducks and geese" to refer to game birds with an official hunting season, but this excludes swans, which are considered waterfowl. Others think the term "waterfowl" refers to all birds that float, but this would include grebes, loons and pelicans and these birds are not waterfowl either.

So, what is it that makes a bird a waterfowl? Waterfowl have common features that define them as waterfowl—large heads, large flattened bills, long necks, short tails and webbed feet.

Other water birds—waterfowl look-alikes—such as the Pied-billed Grebe and Common Loon, are not closely related. A grebe, for example, lacks some of the main characteristics such as a large flattened bill and webbed feet. Grebes are also expert divers and spend much more time underwater than any duck or goose. Their diet is also different from most ducks and geese, consisting mainly of small fish and aquatic insects. Loons are sleek birds that are so well adapted for life in water that they spend 99 percent of their lives either on or under water. They also feed on fish, which is not part of the diet of most ducks, geese and swans.

Waterfowl almost always nest near the water. Most nest on the ground, but several species, such as the Common Goldeneye and Black-bellied Whistling-Duck, nest in artificial cavities or natural holes in trees.

Most waterfowl eggs are dull white or pale olive and do not have any speckles or other markings. All eggs in a clutch hatch at the same time (synchronously). Newly hatched waterfowl will imprint on their parent (often the female), who leads the group to the water to begin a semiaquatic life. This usually occurs within 24-36 hours after hatching.

All water birds share an invaluable feature—an oil or preening gland, called the uropygial gland, located near the base of the tail. This small pimple-like gland secretes an oily substance that the bird picks up with its bill and spreads around (preens) into its feathers. Recent research shows that most bird feathers are at least water resistant simply by design. Structures of a feather work together so that water is channeled off the feathers and not into the body, keeping the bird dry. The oil facilitates waterproofing but only indirectly, making feathers soft, flexible and longer lasting.

PLUMAGES

In most waterfowl, namely ducks, males and females usually do not look the same. This is called sexual dimorphism. Male ducks tend to have brighter colors than the females, which are often overall brown. It is thought the bright colors attract female ducks and show that the males are mature, healthy and ready to breed. Since most male ducks do not incubate or raise young, the bright colors that might attract predators are not a liability to ducklings.

Male and female geese and swans are not sexually dimorphic, so in these groups both sexes look the same. Males stay with their mates, helping to incubate and raise young goslings and cygnets. Most geese and swans remain in small family units for up to a year, with parents staying together possibly for many years.

Like most other birds, waterfowl follow a regular sequence of plumage molts. The timing of the molt for waterfowl, however, may be different from that of other birds. Adult waterfowl have two body plumages per breeding cycle. Most male ducks acquire a colorful breeding plumage in late fall or early winter known as alternate (nuptial) plumage. They retain this plumage until they leave the female ducks just after breeding the following spring.

After breeding, adult male ducks molt back to a duller plumage called basic (eclipse), keeping it for only a few months, from mid-summer to fall. This is the time when wing and tail feathers are replaced, rendering the bird relatively flightless. This is also when male ducks gather in small groups to lay low and avoid predators.

MIGRATION

In Minnesota, most ducks, geese, swans and other water birds are highly migratory, moving in fall to warmer climates where water is not frozen and returning in spring when the ice has melted.

WATERFOWL ANATOMY

These labeled images point out the basic parts of waterfowl. Every attempt has been made to label all parts of the birds with the terminology used in the text; however, not all of the anatomy (terminology) of a water bird has been used in this book.

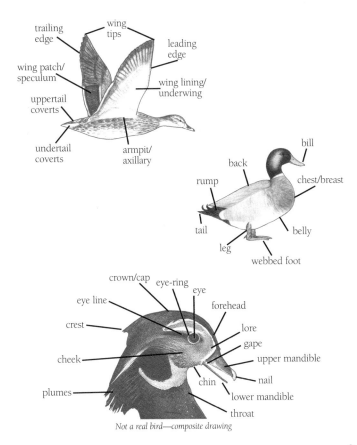

Not a real bird—composite drawing

HOW TO USE THIS BOOK

As discussed on pages 6-7, the scientific classifications of birds found on water can be confusing to the average person. We have therefore elected not to use the technical categories, but instead divide this book into six sections based on characteristics most people will notice. These sections are designated by the following icons and categories in the thumb tabs on each species' page.

| Dabbling Ducks | Diving Ducks | Sea Ducks | Geese | Swans | Other Water Birds |

Dabbling Ducks

You'll easily recognize these ducks by their tails in the air while they feed below the surface of the water, "dabbling" for food.

Diving Ducks

"Divers" quickly dive beneath the surface, submerging to feed at the bottom. They will reappear either in the same place or some distance away.

Sea Ducks

Sea ducks are also diving ducks, but they live in both fresh and salt water, usually migrating to the Pacific or Atlantic coasts, where they sometimes remain at sea for the winter. When seen in Minnesota, they are usually on large bodies of water such as Lake Superior, Lake Mille Lacs or Leech and Upper Red Lakes during migration.

Geese

Most everyone can identify the larger body shape of a goose. You can also spot a goose in flight by noticing the mid-body wing placement, as opposed to the wing location on ducks, which is farther back.

Swans	Swans have large bodies and unmistakable long, curved necks.
Other Water Birds	You'll see these other birds on water and though they are often mistaken for ducks, they are technically not waterfowl. They include grebes, loons and mergansers (even though mergansers are often classified with ducks in other books).

IDENTIFICATION STEP-BY-STEP

If you encounter a bird on the water that you want to identify, we suggest the following steps:

1. If your bird has the easily identifiable shape of a goose or swan, go right to those thumb tabs.

2. If it's not a goose or swan, chances are it's a duck. Notice its feeding pattern—if it dips its head in the water and tips its tail in the air, it's a dabbler. Turn to the Dabbling Ducks section.

3. If the duck completely disappears under the surface, it may be a diver; go directly to the Diving Ducks section. If you don't find it there AND you are on a large body of water, go to the Sea Ducks section.

4. If you don't find your bird in any of these sections, you probably have a waterfowl look-alike, so go to the Other Water Birds section.

Remember that within these sections, species are arranged from small to large so you can refine your search. If you already know the name of the bird, using the index will be most efficient.

Quick Compare Section

To quickly compare species you may find it helpful to go to pages 14-28, where you'll find illustrations that enable you to contrast body and wing shapes, markings and more. Page numbers are indicated so you can verify your bird by going right to its section.

Wild and Domestic Species

While the vast majority of the birds in this book are wild, we've included seven species of domestic ducks, geese and swans. These species have been released into the wild and may be encountered quite frequently in certain areas, and we want the reader to be successful in identifying them. While we've devoted four pages of information for the wild species, we've allotted only two pages for the domestics, simply to facilitate identification.

Photos

Ducks and geese can look very different depending on the sex, age, season or if they are in flight, resting on the ground or swimming. Therefore, we have provided as many variations of photos as possible. Generally, the large main photo depicts the bird on the water. On the following pages, we've tried to show the bird in flight. In the smaller photos, we've also included juveniles, non-breeding adults, displaying males and other variations.

Flight and Flock Patterns

Flight pattern photos and illustrations simply depict the tendency of a flock, not the way it appears every time. These illustrated formations just represent how a flock might look, not how it always looks. Water bird flocks are dynamic, changing constantly. Please use the flight pattern inset as a general guide only.

Range Maps

Included for each bird, these colored maps indicate where in Minnesota a particular bird is most likely to be found during a specific season. Green is used for summer, blue for winter, red for year-round and yellow for areas where the bird is seen during migration. While every effort has been made to accurately depict these ranges, they are only guidelines. Ranges actually change on an ongoing basis due to a variety of factors. Changes in the weather, species abundance, landscape and availability of food and water can affect local populations, migration and movements, causing birds to be found in areas atypical for the species. Please use the maps as intended—as general guides only.

WATER BIRD REHAB

Encounters with birds can involve an injured or orphaned individual. Many well-intentioned people try to care for such a bird, but please, give it the best care it deserves and turn it over to a licensed professional wildlife rehabilitator. Information about the largest wildlife rehab center in the state, Wildlife Rehabilitation Center of Minnesota, is available at www.wrcmn.org.

REGULATIONS AND MANAGEMENT

Hunting and other activities involving migratory birds are regulated by the Minnesota Department of Natural Resources (DNR) and U.S. Fish and Wildlife Service (USFWS). Some species are federally protected from all harvest. Information is available at the DNR main web page at www.dnr.state.mn.us.

It might be noted that since the days of unregulated market hunting ended, hunters have had a huge positive effect on waterfowl populations through excise taxes on hunting equipment ($200 million annually), along with state and federal duck stamps. Since 1934, Minnesota hunters have purchased more than 9 million federal stamps, with sales raising over $700 million nationally, resulting in the purchase of more than 5.2 million acres of habitat.

In addition, local sportsmen's clubs, the Minnesota Waterfowl Association and national organizations, such as Ducks Unlimited and Delta Waterfowl, also work to protect the future of ducks, geese and other wildlife by setting aside thousands of acres of habitat and advocating for conservation legislatively.

POSITIVE IDENTIFICATION

No matter if you are a backyard bird watcher, seasoned birder or veteran hunter, identifying Minnesota's many types of waterfowl can be challenging. Now you have *Ducks & Geese of Minnesota Field Guide* to help you quickly and accurately identify our great water birds. Enjoy the Waterfowl and Other Water Birds!

Stan

Green-winged Teal
(pg. 33)

female

male

male

female

Blue-winged Teal
(pg. 37)

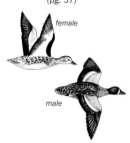

female

male

male

female

Cinnamon Teal
(pg. 41)

female

male

male

female

Mandarin Duck
(pg. 45)

female

male

male

female

Wood Duck
(pg. 47)

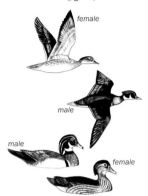

female
male
male
female

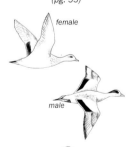

Eurasian Wigeon
(pg. 51)

female
male
male
female

American Wigeon
(pg. 55)

female
male
male
female

Fulvous Whistling-Duck
(pg. 59)

Black-bellied Whistling-Duck
(pg. 63)

Northern Shoveler
(pg. 67)

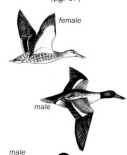

female

male

male

female

Gadwall
(pg. 71)

female

male

male

female

Northern Pintail
(pg. 75)

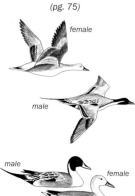

female

male

male

female

QUICK COMPARE

American Black Duck
(pg. 79)

female

male

male *female*

Mallard
(pg. 83)

female

male

male *female*

Domestic Mallard
(pg. 87)

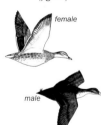
female

male

male *female*

Muscovy Duck
(pg. 89)

Bufflehead
(pg. 91)

female

male

male *female*

Ruddy Duck
(pg. 95)

female

male

male *female*

Ring-necked Duck
(pg. 99)

female

male

male *female*

Lesser Scaup
(pg. 103)

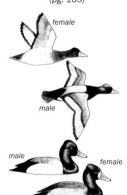

female

male

male *female*

Greater Scaup
(pg. 107)

female

male

male *female*

Barrow's Goldeneye
(pg. 111)

female

male

male   *female*

Common Goldeneye
(pg. 115)

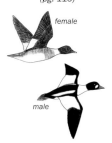

female

male

male   *female*

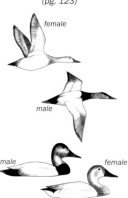

Redhead
(pg. 119)

female

male

male   *female*

Canvasback
(pg. 123)

female

male

male   *female*

19

Harlequin Duck
(pg. 127)

female

male

male

female

Long-tailed Duck
(pg. 131)

female

male

male

female

Black Scoter
(pg. 135)

female

male

male

female

Surf Scoter
(pg. 139)

female

male

male

female

White-winged Scoter
(pg. 143)

female

male

male *female*

King Eider
(pg. 147)

female

male

male *female*

Ross's Goose
(pg. 151)

Cackling Goose
(pg. 155)

Brant
(pg. 159)

Greater White-fronted Goose
(pg. 163)

Snow Goose
(pg. 167)

Canada Goose
(pg. 171)

Graylag Goose
(pg. 175)

Swan Goose
(pg. 177)

Tundra Swan
(pg. 179)

Whooper Swan
(pg. 183)

Mute Swan
(pg. 185)

Trumpeter Swan
(pg. 187)

Eared Grebe
(pg. 191)

Pied-billed Grebe
(pg. 195)

Horned Grebe
(pg. 199)

Red-necked Grebe
(pg. 203)

Western Grebe
(pg. 207)

Clark's Grebe
(pg. 211)

Common Moorhen
(pg. 215)

American Coot
(pg. 219)

Hooded Merganser
(pg. 223)

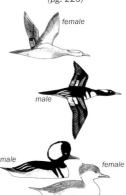

female

male

male   *female*

Red-breasted Merganser
(pg. 227)

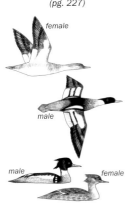

female

male

male   *female*

Common Merganser
(pg. 231)

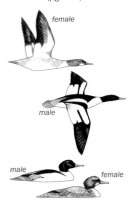

female

male

male   *female*

Red-throated Loon
(pg. 235)

27

Pacific Loon
(pg. 239)

Common Loon
(pg. 243)

Double-crested Cormorant
(pg. 247)

American White Pelican
(pg. 251)

Range Map

Group Tab

DABBLING DUCKS

Common Name

Scientific name   Group Icon

YEAR-ROUND
MIGRATION
SUMMER
WINTER

Size: (L) average length or range of length from head to tail; (WS) average range of wingspan; (WT) average weight or range of weight

Male: brief description of the male bird; may include non-breeding or other plumages

Female: brief description of the female bird, which is sometimes not the same as the male

Juvenile: brief description of the juvenile bird, which often looks like the female

Food: what the bird eats most of the time (e.g., plants, mollusks, crustaceans, tadpoles, fish, insects)

Habitat: environment where the bird is found (e.g., ponds, lakes, rivers, coasts, wetlands, forests, pastures)

Sounds: calls or other vocalizations; may include noises created by activity or other information

Compare: Notes about other birds that look similar and the pages on which they can be found. May include extra information to help identify.

male

Flight: how the bird flies and wing beats; identifying colors and features of the bird seen during flight; may include position of the head, neck or feet

flight pattern

Flock: number of individuals in a flock or number of birds usually seen in flight; shape or formation in flight, including any special characteristics

Migration: complete (regular, seasonal migration patterns), partial (seasonal movement, but destination varies), irruptive (unpredictable movement, depends on the food supply), non-migrator (year-round resident); may include additional information

male   **pair**   **non-breeding male**   **small group**

Nesting: kind of nest the bird builds and the location; who builds the nest and nesting materials; how many broods per year

Eggs/Incubation: number of eggs, color and marking; who does the most incubation and average incubation time

Fledging: average time that young stay in the nest after hatching but before they leave the nest; who does the most "childcare" and feeding; feeding response of young

Stan's Notes: Interesting gee-whiz natural history information. This can be something to look or listen for, or something to help positively identify the bird such as remarkable features, unique behaviors and other key characteristics.

Green-winged Teal
Anas crecca

MIGRATION
SUMMER

Size: L 15" (38 cm); WS 20-24" (50-60 cm); WT 12 oz. (340 g)

Male: Overall gray-to-brown bird with a tan chest. Dark chestnut head with an obvious dark green patch extending from each eye down to nape and outlined with a thin white line. Small, vertical white bar at the shoulder. Black and yellow tail. Small dark bill. Green patch on wings (speculum), seen in flight. Non-breeding (Jul-Sep) is overall brown with fine black spots, appearing like the female.

Female: overall light brown with fine black spots, a small yellow patch at the base of tail, green speculum, dark eye line and small, thin black bill

Juvenile: same as female

Food: aquatic plants and insects, tadpoles, seeds, grains

Habitat: shallow ponds, shallow slow-moving streams

Sounds: female gives a series of squeaky quacks; courting male gives a shrill, high-pitched (piping) call

Compare: Male Green-winged Teal is less colorful than the male Wood Duck (pg. 47). Male American Wigeon (pg. 55) shares the green head patch, but is larger and has a white forehead, rust sides and black tail. The male Blue-winged Teal (pg. 37) is similar in size, but has a dark head and white crescent-shaped mark at the base of its bill. Look for the chestnut head with dark green patches to identify the male Green-winged.

Female Green-winged is very similar to many other duck species. The female Blue-winged Teal (pg. 37) is comparable in size, but it has a small white mark at the base of its bill and blue speculum. Look for the yellow patch on the tail and thin bill to help identify the female Green-winged.

female

Flight: extremely fast, often erratic flight with fast, shallow wing beats; male has a white belly with a darker chest, neck and head, white wing linings, gray wing tips, green wing patch (speculum) and short tail; female appears similar, only slightly darker; feet tuck in during longer flights

flight pattern

Flock: 2-200 individuals; compact, irregularly shaped mass that often turns and twists erratically as one unit, flying low over the surface of water

Migration: complete migrator, to southern states and Mexico

male

female

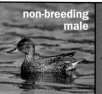
non-breeding male

small group

Nesting: ground, often far from water, sometimes near the edge of water, well concealed in a clump of grass; female builds with grasses, twigs and leaves gathered from the immediate area and lines nest with down feathers plucked from her chest and belly; 1 brood

Eggs/Incubation: 8-10 creamy white eggs; female incubates 21-23 days

Fledging: 32-34 days; female leads young to food; ducklings feed instinctively

Stan's Notes: The Green-winged Teal is the smallest dabbling duck in North America. Usually seen in the northern portion of the state in summer, nesting as far north as Canada and Alaska.

Tips forward in water to feed off the bottom of shallow ponds, or skims insects off the water's surface. Feeding on the bottom makes it vulnerable to ingesting spent lead shot, which can cause death.

This compact bird is known for its fast and agile flight. Flocks spin and wheel through the air in tight formation, green wing patches (speculums) flashing. Walks well on land and often feeds on green plants in fields and woodlands and along the shore.

Usually monogamous, but like Mallards (pg. 83), males will mate with more females than just their partner, engaging them by force. Male usually leaves the female when she starts to incubate.

Young have the fastest growth rates of all North American ducks. Within 24 hours of hatching, ducklings leave the nest, follow their mother and feed by instinct. Green-winged young take their first flight at 35-40 days of age.

Blue-winged Teal
Anas discors

SUMMER

Size: L 15-16" (38-40 cm); WS 22-25" (56-63 cm); WT 13 oz. (369 g)

Male: Plain-looking small brown duck, speckled with black. Gray head shines violet in direct sunlight. Dark bill with a large crescent-shaped white mark at the base. Large blue and white patch on upper surface of wings and a smaller green wing patch (speculum). Black tail and small white patch near rump. Non-breeding (Jul-Oct) is overall brown, appearing nearly identical to the female.

Female: overall brown to gray with a white throat and eye-ring, dark eye line and dark bill with a small white patch at the base

Juvenile: similar to female

Food: aquatic plants and insects, seeds, grains

Habitat: prairie pothole lakes, small lakes, marshes, ponds, slow-moving streams

Sounds: weak whistle-like version of the standard duck quack, usually given only by the female; male gives a series of high-pitched peeps when excited

Compare: The Male Blue-winged is slightly larger than the male Green-winged Teal (pg. 33), which has a brown head with a green patch. The male American Wigeon (pg. 55) has a white forehead and green patch on the head. Male Gadwall (pg. 71) shares the black tail, but is overall gray and lacks the white mark at the base of bill. Look for white crescent-shaped mark on each side of the face to identify the male Blue-winged Teal.

The female Blue-winged looks remarkably like other female duck species. Females will be in close proximity to male Blue-wings. Look for the dark eye line and white eye-ring to help identify.

male

Flight: extremely fast flight with steady wing beats, often gliding on cupped wings; male has a dark body, chest, neck and head, dull white wing linings, obvious blue and white patch on upper surface of wings and a smaller green wing patch (speculum); female looks similar to male; feet tuck in during longer flights

flight pattern

Flock: 2-20 individuals; compact, fast-moving flock that twists and turns, often flying low over the water

Migration: complete migrator, to southern states, Mexico and Central America

male   pair   non-breeding   small group
                                    male

Nesting: ground, near or far from water, well concealed in cattails or tall grasses, often with vegetation hanging over it; female builds with materials gathered from the immediate area and lines the nest with fine plant material and down feathers plucked from her chest and belly; 1 brood

Eggs/Incubation: 8-11 creamy white eggs; female incubates 23-27 days

Fledging: 35-44 days; female leads young to food; ducklings feed instinctively

Stan's Notes: One of the smallest ducks in North America and the second most common breeding duck in Minnesota. A widespread nester that breeds as far north as Alaska, south as far as Texas and across the U.S. from Washington to Maine.

Individuals that breed in Alaska and Canada are some of the longest distance migrating ducks, traveling as far as 7,000 miles (11,270 km). It is estimated that nearly 90 percent of the population winters south of the U.S., but large numbers can also be found in Florida and California. Planting crops and cultivating to pond edges have caused a decline in the population, however.

One of the first duck species to migrate each autumn and among the last to return in spring. Almost always seen in small flocks during breeding season and summer, and forms flocks of up to several hundred individuals in winter. Flight has a characteristic twisting, turning movement. Quickly jumps to flight from the surface of the water.

Known to mate (hybridize) with Cinnamon Teals (pg. 41). Male leaves the female near the end of incubation. Female will perform a distraction display to protect her nest, eggs and young.

male

female

RARE

Cinnamon Teal
Anas cyanoptera

Size: L 16" (40 cm); WS 22-25" (56-63 cm); WT 14 oz. (397 g)

Male: Overall deep cinnamon with a darker cinnamon head and light brown back. Black rump and tail. Blue patch on the upper surface of wings and a smaller green wing patch (speculum). Dark gray bill and deep red eyes. Non-breeding (Jul-Sep) is overall brown with a red tinge.

Female: overall light brown with a plain light brown head, a long, shovel-like dark bill, blue patch on wings and green speculum

Juvenile: similar to female

Food: aquatic plants and insects, seeds

Habitat: shallow wetlands, ponds, small lakes, sloughs

Sounds: female gives a weak high-pitched quack that is similar to the quack of the female Blue-winged Teal (pg. 37); displaying male gives a soft chattering or prattling call

Compare: Male Cinnamon Teal shares the cinnamon sides with the male Northern Shoveler (pg. 67), but Shoveler is larger, with a green head and very large spoon-shaped bill. Male Ruddy Duck (pg. 95) shares the black tail, but has a cinnamon body, bold white markings on its face and a large blue bill. The Male Hooded Merganser (pg. 223) has a similar size and shares the cinnamon sides, but its head is a contrasting black and white.

Female Cinnamon is very similar to the smaller female Green-winged Teal (pg. 33) and Blue-winged Teal (pg. 37), both of which have a dark eye line. Look for the plain light brown head and large dark bill to help identify the female Cinnamon Teal.

male

Flight: extremely fast flight with rapid wing beats, often seen flying close to the ground or over the water; male has a dark body, white wing linings, a light blue patch on forewings and green wing patch (speculum) on trailing edges; female looks very similar to male; feet tuck in during longer flights

flight pattern

Flock: 20-200 individuals; compact, irregularly shaped mass that twists and turns, often flying low over the water

Migration: complete migrator, to the Pacific coast, Texas and Mexico

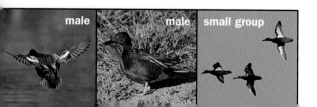

male   male   small group

Nesting: ground, usually within 225 feet (69 m) of the edge of water in a slight depression, well concealed by vegetation; female weaves plant material gathered from the immediate area and lines the nest with bits of grasses and down feathers plucked from her chest and belly; 1 brood

Eggs/Incubation: 7-12 pinkish white eggs; female incubates 21-25 days

Fledging: 40-50 days; female tends young; ducklings copy feeding behavior of mother

Stan's Notes: An uncommon teal in Minnesota, with only a few sightings reported annually. The male is a stunningly beautiful duck, appearing dark brown in low light and nearly neon red in bright sunlight. The unique coloring makes the male Cinnamon Teal one of the most easily recognizable ducks in North America.

Unlike other dabbling ducks that tip forward to reach the bottom to feed, this teal skims the surface of water for aquatic insects and gathers plants just under the surface, close to shore.

Usually seen here only during migration with other duck species. Does not breed in Minnesota, preferring to nest along alkaline marshes and shallow lakes in western states. Hybridizes with the Blue-winged Teal (pg. 37).

The Mallard (pg. 83) and other ducks often lay their eggs in teal nests, resulting in over 15 eggs in many nests. When threatened, the female will feign a wing injury to lure predators away while her ducklings scatter and hide.

male

female

Mandarin Duck
Aix galericulata

DOMESTIC

Size: L 18" (45 cm); WS 27-29" (69-74 cm); WT 1 lb. 1 oz. (.5 kg)

Male: A colorful small duck with distinctive rust cheek feathers. Long drooping crest of rust, black and white. Rust chest. Yellow sides. White belly. Small orange bill with a light tip (nail). Handsome rust "sail" feathers. Blue green wing patch (speculum).

Female: overall brown with large white spots on the sides and chest, distinctive white eye-ring, short crest, small bill with a light nail, blue green speculum

Juvenile: similar to female

Food: aquatic insects, plants, seeds, acorns, berries

Habitat: shallow ponds, small lakes, parks, farms

Sounds: unknown

Compare: Male Mandarin has a similar size as male Wood Duck (pg. 47), with comparable proportions. Male Wood Duck has a green head and lacks the large cheek and "sail" feathers.

Female Mandarin is extremely similar to the female Wood Duck (pg. 47), but is overall lighter brown with larger white spots on sides and chest. To identify, look for a male Mandarin nearby.

Stan's Notes: A non-native species originally from China and Japan, sometimes called Chinese Mandarin Duck. Often raised on hobby farms and irresponsibly released on lakes in city parks. Usually remains in one area, but during winter will move around Minnesota or migrate only far enough south to find open water. Has been known to fly as far as 500 miles (225 km) in one day. Held in high esteem in many Eastern cultures and regarded as a symbol of happiness and fidelity. Not hunted in Asia, apparently because of its unappealing taste. *Domestic species—2 pages only*

male

female

Wood Duck
Aix sponsa

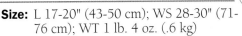

Size: L 17-20" (43-50 cm); WS 28-30" (71-76 cm); WT 1 lb. 4 oz. (.6 kg)

SUMMER

Male: Highly ornamented small duck with a rounded head. Drooping green crest patterned with white and black. Rust chest, yellow sides and white belly. Small tricolored bill, mostly reddish with some white and a black tip. Red eyes. Long dark tail, held upright at an angle. Non-breeding (Jun-Sep) lacks the bright coloring on head and crest.

Female: similar size and shape as the male, overall brown with a less obvious crest, small white spots on the sides and chest, bright white eye-ring, blue patch on wings, often hidden

Juvenile: similar to female

Food: aquatic insects, plants, seeds, acorns, berries

Habitat: woodland ponds, small lakes, shallow backwater lakes and slow-moving rivers in woodlands

Sounds: female gives a familiar drawn-out "oo-eek" when alarmed or to reveal her presence, and squeals loudly during takeoff; displaying male and males in male groups give a short high-pitched whistle

Compare: Male Wood Duck has a similar size as male Hooded Merganser (pg. 223), but Hoodie has a white patch on its head. Male Mandarin Duck (pg. 45) shares the rust chest, yellow sides and white belly, but has distinctive rust cheek and "sail" feathers.

Female Wood Duck is very similar to the female Mandarin Duck (pg. 45) and difficult to distinguish, but the Mandarin has larger white spots on its sides and chest. Female Mallard (pg. 83) and female Blue-winged Teal (pg. 37) are also similar, but lack the bright white eye-ring and crest.

female

Flight: fast direct flight with rapid, shallow wing beats, frequently twisting and turning when flying through woods; male has a white belly with a dark neck, head and tail (appears to have a short neck with a large head) and gray wing linings; female has a white belly with a gray chest, neck and head and speckled gray wing linings; feet tuck in during longer flights

flight pattern

Flock: 2-20 individuals; pairs or a small, tight, fast-moving flock that often twists and turns through the woods

Migration: complete migrator, to southern states

displaying male | female | juvenile male

Nesting: cavity, near the water in a tree cavity, old woodpecker hole or wooden box; female lines the cavity with down feathers plucked from her chest and belly; 1 brood

Eggs/Incubation: 10-15 creamy white eggs; female incubates 28-36 days

Fledging: 56-68 days; female leads young to food; ducklings feed instinctively

Stan's Notes: The male Wood Duck is considered by many to be the most beautiful duck in North America. Nearly extinct around 1900 due to overhunting, but doing well now due to thousands of man-made nest boxes put up by hunters and birders. Once exclusively nested in old woodpecker holes and natural cavities in trees, but now half to three-quarters of the population nests in man-made boxes.

A common dabbler of quiet, shallow backwater ponds and small lakes. Frequently seen flying deep in forests or perched high up on tree branches.

Female often enters the nest cavity from full flight, seeming to have disappeared suddenly or to have flown directly into the side of a tree. The female will lay some of her eggs in a neighboring female nest (egg dumping), resulting in 20 or more eggs in some clutches. The eggs at the bottom of such a nest rarely hatch due to the lack of uniform heating.

Young remain in the nest 24 hours after hatching. At the urging of their mother, ducklings jump as far as 30 feet (9 m) to the ground or water to follow her and never return to the nest. Some mothers nest as far as 1 mile (1.6 km) from water and walk their ducklings all the way there and back.

male

female

Eurasian Wigeon
Anas penelope

RARE

Size: L 19" (48 cm); WS 30-32" (76-80 cm);
WT 1 lb. 8 oz. (.7 kg)

Male: Gray duck with a small, rounded reddish head, pale yellow forehead and pointed black tail. Short, light blue-to-grayish bill with a black tip (nail). Non-breeding (Jul-Sep) lacks the yellow forehead and has rust sides.

Female: light brown-to-gray bird, contrasting brown face, short grayish bill with a black tip and small black mark at corners of bill (gape), green wing patch (speculum)

Juvenile: similar to female, with grayer sides and lacking the head color contrast

Food: aquatic plants and insects, seeds, grasses, snails

Habitat: small lakes, ponds, marshes

Sounds: female gives a low quack and makes a growling noise; male gives a distinctive 2- or 3-part whistle

Compare: The Eurasian Wigeon is a very uncommon duck. The male Eurasian is the same size as male American Wigeon (pg. 55), but the American has a green patch on its head and neck and white forehead. Check for the rounded rust head and gray sides to help identify the male Eurasian Wigeon.

The female Eurasian is nearly identical to the female American Wigeon (pg. 55), but the American is browner overall and has a pale gray head.

male

Flight: fast direct flight with fast, shallow wing beats; male has a white belly, brown chest and neck, dark reddish head, gray wing linings and green and white patches on wings; female looks very similar to male, but lacks the bold white patch on the upper surface of wings; feet tuck in during longer flights

flight pattern

Flock: 1-2 individuals, in mixed flocks with American Wigeons or other duck species; tight, irregularly shaped mass that makes many twists and turns

Migration: complete migrator, to the Atlantic and Pacific coasts

male

Nesting: ground, often far from the water, well concealed by tall vegetation; female builds with grasses and weeds gathered from the immediate area and lines the nest with down feathers plucked from her chest and belly; 1 brood

Eggs/Incubation: 7-12 white eggs; female incubates 23-25 days

Fledging: 37-48 days; female tends young; ducklings copy feeding behavior of mother

Stan's Notes: This is a rare dabbling duck, with only one or two showing up in Minnesota each year. Not known to nest regularly in North America. Nests near Nome, Alaska, almost every year and probably in other locations in Alaska, which accounts for the large number of hybrid wigeons in western North America.

Often associated with American Wigeons (pg. 55) or other duck species in mixed flocks. Easily differentiated from the American Wigeon in flight by its gray wing linings and the reddish head of the male.

A dabbling duck, tipping forward in shallow water to feed on aquatic plants, seeds, snails and insects. Walks well on land and often forages for green grass in fields or along the shoreline.

Monogamous, but nests in small colonies. Ducklings leave the nest shortly after hatching and find their own food by following their mother and copying her feeding behavior. Young Eurasians take their first flight at 60-70 days of age.

male

female

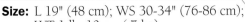

American Wigeon
Anas americana

MIGRATION
SUMMER

Size: L 19" (48 cm); WS 30-34" (76-86 cm); WT 1 lb. 10 oz. (.7 kg)

Male: Brown duck with a small rounded head, obvious white forehead and deep green patch starting at each eye and streaking down the neck. Pointed black tail. Short, light blue-to-grayish bill with a black tip (nail). Non-breeding (Jul-Sep) lacks the white forehead and green head patch.

Female: light brown with a pale gray head, dark eye spot, short grayish bill with a black tip and small black mark at corners of bill (gape), green wing patch (speculum)

Juvenile: similar to female, with a distinctive head-to-body color contrast

Food: aquatic plants and insects, seeds, grasses

Habitat: small lakes, ponds, marshes

Sounds: female gives a low quack and makes a growling noise; male gives a distinctive 2- or 3-part whistle

Compare: The male American Wigeon is the same size as the male Eurasian Wigeon (pg. 51), which has a rust head, yellowish forehead and is extremely uncommon. Male Gadwall (pg. 71) has a brown head, dark gray bill and is slightly larger. The male Green-winged Teal (pg. 33) shares the green head patch, but has gray sides, lacks the white forehead and is smaller.

The female American is nearly identical to the female Eurasian Wigeon (pg. 51), but the Eurasian is slightly grayer overall and has a brown face. Female American resembles the females of many other duck species. Check for the pale gray head and short, black-tipped gray bill to help identify the female American Wigeon.

male

Flight: fast direct flight with fast, shallow wing beats; male has a white belly, brown chest and neck, dark head, white wing linings, gray wing tips, bold white patch on wings and smaller green wing patch (speculum); female is similar, with smaller white patches on wings; juvenile is similar to adult, lacks white wing patches; feet tuck in during longer flights

flight pattern

Flock: 20-200 individuals; tight, irregularly shaped mass that makes many twists and turns

Migration: complete migrator, to southern states and the Atlantic, Pacific and Gulf coasts

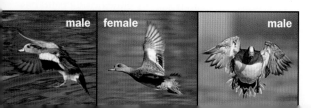
male female male

Nesting: ground, often far from the water, well concealed by tall vegetation; female builds with grasses and weeds gathered from the immediate area and lines the nest with down feathers plucked from her chest and belly; 1 brood

Eggs/Incubation: 7-12 white eggs; female incubates 23-25 days

Fledging: 37-48 days; female tends young; ducklings copy feeding behavior of mother

Stan's Notes: This duck is often called Baldpate by hunters due to its conspicuous white forehead. Frequently in flocks of various sizes or with other duck species. More common in western states, but apparently expanding its range eastward, possibly a result of an increased number of wetlands and nesting sites.

Prefers shallow lakes, ponds and marshes, where it can easily reach the bottom to feed. Feeds by tipping forward at the water's surface or just below it (dabbling). Also grazes on grasses along the shore or in fields.

A monogamous bird that nests alone on dry land, sometimes on islands. Builds an upland nest within 150-750 feet (46-229 m) of the water, concealing it in tall vegetation.

Male stays with the female for the first week or two of incubation only. The female incubates eggs and raises the young by herself. When threatened, the female feigns injury while the young swim away and hide.

Fulvous Whistling-Duck
Dendrocygna bicolor

RARE

Size: L 19-20" (48-50 cm); WS 24-26" (60-66 cm); WT 1 lb. 8 oz. (.7 kg)

Male: Overall tan to light brown with very dark wings and back. White rump and white edges of wings. Long gray legs and gray bill. Dark eyes. Unique posture when standing, holding its long neck in a vertical position.

Female: same as male

Juvenile: dull brown-to-gray body with a gray bill, legs and feet, back is not as dark as the back of adult

Food: seeds, grains, green plants, corn

Habitat: ponds, marshes, slow-moving streams

Sounds: both sexes give a high-pitched wheezy whistle that sounds like air blowing through a hollow tube, usually during flight

Compare: The Fulvous shares the overall shape and posture of the Black-bellied Whistling-Duck (pg. 63), but the Black-bellied is larger, with a rusty red chest and neck, black sides and belly and obvious red-to-orange bill.

A very uncommon duck in Minnesota. The Fulvous appears very tall and thin when standing on land. Its erect posture and long neck and legs differentiate it from most other ducks. Look for the gray bill and white wing edges to help identify this bird.

Flight: direct flight with strong, rapid wing beats; both sexes have a tan belly and neck, dark wings and white rump; juvenile is similar to adult; legs and feet extend beyond the tail

Flock: 2-10 individuals, in mixed flocks with other duck species; irregularly shaped mass, sometimes in straight-line formation

Migration: partial to non-migrator; occasionally appears in Minnesota with other duck species; usually has escaped from captivity or was released

flight pattern

Nesting: cup, in dry fields up to a half mile from the water, on the ground; female and male weave plant material gathered from the immediate area and line the nest with grasses; 1 brood

Eggs/Incubation: 12-16 creamy white eggs; female and male incubate 24-26 days

Fledging: 55-63 days; parents lead young to food; ducklings copy feeding behavior of parents

Stan's Notes: A rare non-native duck in the state. Most records show it occurring in the early to mid-1900s, with its appearance here considered accidental. Usually has escaped from captivity or was released into the wild. Sometimes seen with other wild ducks, or domestic ducks that have also escaped or were released.

Formerly known as Fulvous Tree Duck because it perches in trees. Prefers shallow freshwater ponds and lakes. Can be seen feeding in flooded agricultural fields, and often feeds at night.

In all duck species in North America except two, the female looks different from the male (sexually dimorphic). The Fulvous is one of the two duck species that is not sexually dimorphic. Like the Black-bellied Whistling-Duck (pg. 63), the Fulvous female looks the same as the male.

Breeds in southern parts of Florida, California and Texas. A monogamous species, with mates remaining together possibly for many years. Sometimes the female will lay her eggs in the nest of another female. Both sexes share the task of incubating the eggs and caring for the young—not a common practice among ducks. Behavior is more like a goose than a duck.

Black-bellied Whistling-Duck
Dendrocygna autumnalis

RARE

Size: L 20-22" (50-56 cm); WS 30-34" (76-86 cm); WT 1 lb. 14 oz. (.8 kg)

Male: Overall rusty red to brown with a gray face and upper neck. Black sides, belly and tail. Bold white stripe on the upper surface of wings. Large, long red-to-orange bill with a gray tip (nail). Dark eyes. White eye-ring. Long pink legs and feet. Unique posture when standing, holding its long neck in a vertical position.

Female: same as male

Juvenile: dull brown-to-gray body with a gray bill, legs and feet, lacks the black sides, belly and tail of adult

Food: seeds, grains, aquatic insects, snails

Habitat: ponds, marshes, slow-moving streams

Sounds: both sexes give a high-pitched wheezy whistle that sounds like air blowing through a hollow tube, usually during flight

Compare: The Black-bellied Whistling-Duck shares the rusty red color of the male Cinnamon Teal (pg. 41), but is larger and has black sides, a long neck and reddish orange bill.

Extremely uncommon in Minnesota. Look for the gray face, red-to-orange bill and black sides to help identify this attractive duck. Also look for its unique posture when standing on land, holding its long neck in a straight vertical position.

Flight: direct flight with strong, rapid wing beats; both sexes have a black belly, brown lower neck, gray head and black wings with a large white stripe over the upper surface; juvenile is similar to adult, with a gray belly; legs and feet extend beyond tail

flight pattern

Flock: 2-20 individuals, in mixed flocks with other duck species; irregularly shaped mass, sometimes in straight-line formation

Migration: partial to non-migrator; it occasionally appears in Minnesota with other duck species; usually has escaped from captivity or was released

adult   juvenile small group

Nesting: cavity, in woodlands up to a half mile from the water, in an old woodpecker hole or wooden box; not lined with nesting material; 1 brood

Eggs/Incubation: 12-14 creamy white eggs; female and male incubate 25-30 days

Fledging: 53-63 days; parents lead young to food; ducklings copy feeding behavior of parents

Stan's Notes: A rare duck species in Minnesota, its appearance considered accidental in the state. The last official record of it was in October 1984, when one was shot at Rice Lake in Faribault County. Common in the tropics of Mexico and Central America and normally found in extreme southern Texas, Arizona and parts of Florida.

Usually has escaped from captivity or was released into the wild. Sometimes seen with other wild ducks, or domestic ducks that also have escaped or were released. Occasionally found in ponds and woodlands in city parks, where people introduced it into the environment. Also may be seen swimming in pairs or small flocks in shallow woodland ponds, or perching in trees. Nests in tree cavities, but also will use man-made nest boxes similar to Wood Duck (pg. 47) boxes. Often feeds at night and will retreat into woodlands when disturbed.

In all duck species in North America except two, the female looks different from the male (sexually dimorphic). The Black-bellied is one of the two duck species that is not sexually dimorphic. Like the Fulvous Whistling-Duck (pg. 59), the Black-bellied female looks the same as the male.

A monogamous breeder. Both sexes incubate eggs and care for the young, an uncommon practice among ducks. The female will "dump" her eggs in the nests of other females, which results in clutches of several dozen eggs.

male

female

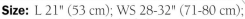
Northern Shoveler
Anas clypeata

Size: L 21" (53 cm); WS 28-32" (71-80 cm);
WT 1 lb. 4 oz. (.6 kg)

MIGRATION
SUMMER

Male: Iridescent green head and neck, rust red sides
and a bright white chest. Extraordinarily large
spoon-shaped dark bill. Light blue patch on the
upper surface of wings and a smaller green wing
patch (speculum), seen during flight. Pointed
dark tail. Yellow eyes. Non-breeding (Jul-Nov)
has varying amounts of green on head, mottled
rust sides and very little white on the chest.

Female: light brown duck speckled with black, extremely
large spoon-shaped orange and gray bill, green
speculum, orange legs and feet

Juvenile: similar to female

Food: aquatic plants and insects, clams, snails

Habitat: shallow freshwater ponds and marshes, prairie
pothole lakes, small shallow lakes

Sounds: female gives a weak quack; courting male gives a
series of stuttering calls that sounds like "tok tok
tok tok tok"

Compare: Male Northern Shoveler is similar to the male Mallard
(pg. 83), but Mallard lacks the rusty red sides and bright white
chest. Male Common Merganser (pg. 231) also lacks rusty sides
and is larger, with a thin orange bill. Male Wood Duck (pg. 47)
is smaller and has a crest.

Female Northern Shoveler is similar to the females of many other
duck species. The female Mallard (pg. 83) is similar in color, but
lacks a large spoon-shaped bill. Look for the very large bill and
green speculum of the female Northern Shoveler.

male

Flight: strong direct flight with rapid, shallow wing beats; male has a rust belly, black tail, white chest, green neck and white-to-gray wing linings, with a light blue patch on upper surface of wings and smaller green wing patch (speculum); female is overall light brown with white wing linings and green speculum; feet tuck in during longer flights

flight pattern

Flock: 20-200 individuals; irregular V shape or in a tight cluster

Migration: complete migrator, to southern states, the Gulf coast, Mexico and Central America

non-breeding male   female   feeding pair   small group

Nesting: ground, near the edge of water in short grass, in a slight depression; female fills depression with dried grasses and other vegetation gathered from the immediate area and lines nest with down feathers plucked from her chest and belly; 1 brood

Eggs/Incubation: 9-12 olive eggs; female incubates 22-25 days

Fledging: 30-60 days; female leads young to food; ducklings feed instinctively

Stan's Notes: No other duck species in North America has a bill as large as the Northern Shoveler. Frequently just called Shoveler, referring to the peculiar shape of its bill. Sometimes mistakenly called Spoonbill.

A large diving duck of shallow marshes, ponds and lakes. Usually holds its head low when swimming, pointing its bill toward the surface of water or partially submerging it into the water. Often uses its bill to skim the water's surface while swimming, using the comb-like teeth along the sides of the bill to strain water from tiny aquatic plants and other food it collects. Mated pairs often feed together, submerging their bills and circling repeatedly to stir up the muddy bottom and unearth food.

Springs to flight from the surface of the water and is a swift flyer, occasionally darting back and forth in teal-like fashion before it turns and lands. Usually seen in small flocks of 5-10 birds except during migration, when it can be found in larger numbers.

A monogamous breeder, often one of the last ducks to nest each year. Females are sporadic incubators, spending more time away from the nest than other duck species, foraging for food. Some males will remain with the females while they incubate, but most abandon the females at that time and do not help raise the young.

male

female

Gadwall

Anas strepera

YEAR-ROUND
MIGRATION
SUMMER

Size: L 21" (53 cm); WS 32-35" (80-88 cm); WT 2 lb. (.9 kg)

Male: Plump gray duck with a brown head. Distinctive black rump and tail. Chestnut-tinged wings and bright white wing linings. Small white wing patch (speculum), visible when swimming. White belly. Small dark gray bill. Non-breeding (Jun-Aug) is overall brown with a gray head and orange and black bill.

Female: mottled brown with a pronounced color change from a light brown head and neck to dark brown body, bright white wing linings, small white patch on wings, visible when swimming, small dark bill with yellow-to-orange edges

Juvenile: similar to female

Food: aquatic plants and insects, grasses, seeds

Habitat: ponds, shallow marshes, small lakes

Sounds: female gives a harsher and perhaps more nasal quack than that of female Mallard; courting male gives a low sharp call followed by wheezy sounds and whistles

Compare: The male Gadwall is one of the few gray ducks. The male Northern Pintail (pg. 75) is larger, with a white chest and long thin tail. The male American Wigeon (pg. 55) is smaller and has a white forehead and green patch on its head. Look for the distinctive black rump of the male Gadwall.

Female Gadwall is very similar to the females of many other duck species. Look for the white patch on the wings and dark bill with yellow-to-orange edges to help identify the female Gadwall.

male

Flight: fast direct flight with rapid wing beats; male has a distinct white belly, dark chest, neck and tail and bright white wing linings, with a distinctive black patch on upper surface of wings and smaller white wing patch (speculum); female is very similar to male; feet tuck in during longer flights

flight pattern

Flock: 2-20 individuals; compact, irregularly shaped flock, sometimes in straight-line formation

Migration: complete migrator, to southern states and Mexico

male   female   female   non-breeding male

Nesting: ground, up to 300 feet (91 m) from the edge of water, well concealed by dense grasses and tall reeds; female builds with plant material gathered from the immediate area and lines the nest with fine grasses and down feathers plucked from her chest and belly; 1 brood

Eggs/Incubation: 8-11 white eggs; female incubates 24-27 days

Fledging: 48-56 days; female tends young; ducklings copy feeding behavior of mother

Stan's Notes: Also called Gray Duck or Gray Mallard. Relatively uncommon, this dabbling duck of shallow marshes is often seen in mixed flocks with other duck species such as Mallard (pg. 83) and Northern Pintail (pg. 75). Usually shy and wary, moving around in small flocks of fewer than 20 birds.

Consumes mostly plant material, dunking its head into water to feed rather than tipping forward, like the other dabbling ducks. Walks well on land, feeding on grasses in fields and along shorelines. When on land, it feeds farther away from the water than other dabbling ducks.

The Gadwall breeding season occurs later than that of most other ducks. Pair bond is established in winter, when the male displays for the female by raising his tail out of the water and shows off his wing patch (speculum) while bobbing his head.

Females have a tenacity for the nest site and will lay eggs in other Gadwall nests (nest parasitism). Successful hatching is frequently greater in Gadwalls than in other duck species. Young leave the nest shortly after hatching and follow their mother to the water, where they watch what she eats and copy her example.

male

female

Northern Pintail
Anas acuta

MIGRATION
SUMMER

Size: L 21-25" (53-63 cm); WS 33-35" (84-88 cm); WT 1 lb. 14 oz. (.8 kg)

Male: A slender, elegant duck with a brown head, gray body and extremely long, narrow black tail. Long white neck with a white stripe extending up the sides of head. Narrow gray and black bill. Non-breeding (Jul-Oct) is overall gray to brown with no clear color demarcation between the brown head and white neck. Lacks long tail feathers.

Female: mottled brown body with a paler brown head and neck, long pointed tail and narrow gray bill

Juvenile: similar to female

Food: aquatic plants and insects, minnows, tadpoles, seeds

Habitat: small lakes, ponds, woodland ponds, marshes

Sounds: female gives a series of descending quacks along with a rapid series of short stuttering quacks that make it sound like laughter, calls are like those of female Mallard, but softer and hoarser; courting male gives a flutey call with soft wheezy notes

Compare: Male Northern Pintail shares the black tail with male Gadwall (pg. 71), but Gadwall lacks the brown head and white chest and neck. Check for the long white neck, brown head and extremely long tail feathers to help identify the male Pintail.

Female Northern Pintail is similar to female Mallard (pg. 83), but Mallard has an orange bill with black spots. The female Gadwall (pg. 71) is similar in size, but lacks a long neck and has yellow orange edges on its bill. Look for the long neck, long tail feathers and narrow gray bill to help identify the female Pintail.

male

Flight: fast direct flight with fast, full wing beats; male has a white belly, chest and neck, gray wing linings; female has a light brown-to-tan body with gray wing linings; long outstretched neck and long tail feathers are obvious during flight, feet tuck in during longer flights

flight pattern

Flock: 20-200 individuals; irregularly shaped flock, sometimes in straight-line formation, flying high in the sky and descending rapidly in a characteristic zigzag pattern

Migration: complete migrator, to southern states and Mexico

male   female   non-breeding male

Nesting: ground, up to 100 feet (30 m) from the edge of water, concealed by tall grasses; female builds with grasses, leaves and other plant materials gathered from the immediate area and lines the nest with down feathers from her chest and belly; 1 brood

Eggs/Incubation: 6-9 olive green eggs; female incubates 22-25 days

Fledging: 36-50 days; female leads young to food; ducklings feed instinctively

Stan's Notes: No other North American duck has such a long tail. Male holds its tail upright from the water's surface, making it one of the easiest ducks to identify in low light. The long tail and neck make it appear larger than the Mallard (pg. 83), but its body size is slightly smaller and it weighs less. One of the few duck species in which the male is obviously larger than the female, not including the tail.

One of the easiest ducks to identify in flight by its long slender body, long outstretched neck and long tail. Often flies very high in the sky, quickly descending in a unique zigzag pattern before coming to rest on the water's surface.

A common dabbling duck of shallow marshes. About 90 percent of its diet is aquatic plants, except when the female feeds heavily on aquatic insects prior to nesting, presumably to gain additional nutrients for egg production.

Monogamous and a solitary nester. Only the female attends the young. Ducklings leave the nest within hours of hatching and take their first flight at 50-60 days of age.

Population has declined since around 1905. More common in western states and not found in huge numbers in any one place in Minnesota.

male

female

American Black Duck
Anas rubripes

YEAR-ROUND
MIGRATION
SUMMER
WINTER

Size: L 23" (58 cm); WS 34-36" (86-90 cm);
WT 2 lb. 10 oz. (1.2 kg)

Male: Heavy-bodied duck with a distinct color contrast from head and neck to body. Overall dark brown, sometimes appearing nearly black, with a lighter head and neck. Dark eye line, extending to the back of head. Yellowish bill with a black tip (nail). Orange legs and feet. Violet patch on the wings (speculum), bordered with black.

Female: same as male, but dull green bill with black flecks

Juvenile: same as female

Food: aquatic plants and insects, seeds, snails, berries

Habitat: ponds and small lakes in woodlands, wetlands

Sounds: female gives a series of loud descending quacks along with a rapid series of short stuttering quacks that make it sound like laughter; female call is a familiar one, nearly identical to the call of female Mallard, but can be slightly weaker and softer; courting male gives a soft grunt whistle along with a soft quack

Compare: The male and female American Black Ducks are very similar to the female and non-breeding (eclipse) male Mallard (pg. 83). Female Mallard has an orange bill and blue wing patch with a white border. The non-breeding (eclipse) male Mallard has a gray head with a brighter yellow bill than the male Black Duck.

Look for the sharp color change from the lighter head and neck to the darker body to help identify the male and female American Black Duck.

male

Flight: fast direct flight with strong wing beats; both sexes have a dark body and bright white wing linings, both lack white on the upper surface of the wings, but have a violet wing patch (speculum); feet tuck in during longer flights

flight pattern

Flock: 2-20 individuals; irregularly shaped small groups that usually fly high over the water and drop down suddenly to make a landing

Migration: complete migrator, to central and southern states

male   **male**   **pair**

Nesting: ground, near the edge of water, concealed by tall grass; female builds with dried grasses gathered from the immediate area and lines the nest with fine plants and down feathers plucked from her chest and belly; 1 brood

Eggs/Incubation: 8-10 creamy white-to-greenish buff eggs; female incubates 26-29 days

Fledging: 17 days; female tends young; ducklings copy feeding behavior of mother

Stan's Notes: Prior to 1940, this was one of the most abundant ducks breeding in the U.S. and also the most heavily hunted. Its numbers today in the eastern half of the country have dropped dramatically to the point of absence of this species in some areas. Its decline may have developed from a combination of overhunting, loss of woodland habitat and displacement by the Mallard (pg. 83), now the most common duck species in North America.

A monogamous breeder and solitary nester. Occasionally mates (hybridizes) with Mallards, producing birds that lack the brilliant colors of the male Mallard.

Male leaves the female while she is still incubating the eggs and will have nothing to do with raising the young. Ducklings leave the nest 1-3 hours after hatching and follow their mother to water, where they immediately start to feed by instinct.

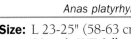

Mallard
Anas platyrhynchos

DABBLING DUCKS

YEAR-ROUND
SUMMER

Size: L 23-25" (58-63 cm); WS 33-35" (84-88 cm); WT 2 lb. - 2 lb. 6 oz. (.9-1.1 kg)

Male: Large, bulbous green head, white necklace and rust brown or chestnut chest. Gray and white on the sides. Yellow bill. Orange legs and feet. Non-breeding (Jun-Sep) is overall brown with a dark eye line and dull yellow bill; some non-breeding (eclipse) males have a gray head.

Female: brown duck, orange bill with black patches in the center, blue wing patch (speculum) with a white border, dark eye line

Juvenile: same as female, but has a yellow bill

Food: seeds, plants, aquatic insects, comes to ground feeders containing corn

Habitat: wetlands, ponds, lakes, slow-moving rivers

Sounds: female gives a familiar series of loud descending quacks along with a rapid series of short stuttering quacks that make it sound like laughter; courting male gives a soft grunt whistle

Compare: Male Mallard is larger than male Northern Shoveler (pg. 67), which has a white chest and rust sides. The male Red-breasted Merganser (pg. 227) has a shaggy crest and orange bill. Domestic Mallard (pg. 87) is overall darker. The male Northern Pintail (pg. 75) has a brown head and long tail feathers.

Female Mallard is larger than female Blue-winged Teal (pg. 37). The female Wood Duck (pg. 47) is smaller, with a white eye-ring. Female Northern Shoveler (pg. 67) has a large spoon-shaped bill. The female Gadwall (pg. 71) is similar, but has a white wing patch and small dark bill with yellow orange edges. The female Northern Pintail (pg. 75) has a long pointed tail and gray bill.

83

male

Flight: fast direct flight with slower, shallower wing beats than other ducks; male has a light gray-to-white belly, brown chest and neck, white wing linings and gray wing tips; female has a nearly all-brown belly, white wing linings and gray wing tips; feet tuck in during longer flights

flight pattern

Flock: 3-300 individuals; tight flock, round mass or no particular shape, often "blasting off" from the water's surface

Migration: complete migrator, to southern states; small percentage remain in Minnesota during winter

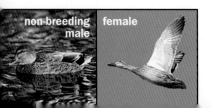

non-breeding male

female

Nesting: platform, near the edge of water, on the ground; female builds with a small amount of plant material gathered from the immediate area and lines the nest with down feathers plucked from her chest and belly; 1 brood

Eggs/Incubation: 7-10 greenish eggs; female incubates 26-30 days

Fledging: 42-52 days; female leads young to food; ducklings feed instinctively

Stan's Notes: One of the most widespread duck species in North America. A familiar duck of lakes and ponds, found just about anywhere fresh water is available. Some also live in salt water. The male Mallard has black central tail feathers that curl upward, a characteristic unique to this species. One of the few duck species in which the males are noticeably larger than females. Also known as Greenhead.

Considered a type of dabbling duck, tipping forward in shallow water to feed on plants, but sometimes dives completely underwater when bathing or during courtship. Prone to lead poisoning when spent lead shot is ingested from the lake bottom.

Males molt from midsummer to late summer, appearing nearly the same as the females. During their seasonal molt, both sexes are rendered flightless for up to 30 days. Mates with one partner each season (seasonally monogamous), with some pairs remaining together for several years. Female leads ducklings to water after hatching. Young return to birthplace.

"Mallard" is from the Latin *masculus*, meaning "male," and refers to the male habit of non-participation in the raising of young.

Many varieties of Domestic Mallard (pg. 87) can be found in the wild, usually the result of someone raising and releasing the birds. This is not a good practice because it introduces non-native birds into the environment that compete with wild birds for a limited supply of food.

white-necked
male

black

white

female

Domestic Mallard

Anas platyrhynchos

DOMESTIC

Size: L 24" (60 cm); WS 34" (86 cm); WT 2.5-
3 lb. (1.1-1.4 kg)

Male: Overall dark brown to black with a white chest
and neck. Bill is dull yellow to dull orange. Legs
and feet are dull orange to dull yellow. Can have
a green head. May be partly to mostly white with
a dull orange bill.

Female: brown with dark markings, bill is dull green to
dull yellow, dull orange legs and feet, blue patch
on wings (speculum) with white edging

Juvenile: similar to female

Food: aquatic plants and insects, grains, seeds, grasses

Habitat: barnyards, city parks and ponds, petting zoos,
lakes, rivers

Sounds: female gives familiar loud quacking calls and
funny laughing calls; male gives short rasping
calls and whistles during breeding season

Compare: The male Mallard (pg. 83) has a bright green head,
chestnut brown chest and black and white tail. Female Mallard
(pg. 83) is extremely similar to the female Domestic Mallard, but
there are dark markings on the wild female's orange bill.

Stan's Notes: The first breeds of Domestic Mallard were bred for
food and body size. These birds are easy to spot due to their large
thick bodies, up to twice the size of wild Mallards. Wild Mallards
are the ancestors of Domestic Mallards. Domestics can breed with
wild Mallards, resulting in a variety of offspring. Seen in a wide
range of colors including an all-white variety that is also known
as Pekin Duck. Often found with others of its kind in city parks
with ponds or lakes, usually a result of someone irresponsibly
releasing their ducks into the wild. *Domestic species—2 pages only*

male

female

white/black

Muscovy Duck
Cairina moschata

DOMESTIC

Size: L 28" (71 cm); WS 46-48" (117-120 cm);
WT 5-10 lb. (2.3-4.5 kg)

Male: Bumpy patch of red flesh (caruncle) around eyes
and bill. Typically black and white, mostly white,
brown, blue or a combination of colors. Some
exhibit wild coloration of glossy green-black with
a warty face, short dark bill and white wing patch.
Most of the colored varieties have a white patch
on wings.

Female: same as male, but up to half the size, no caruncle

Juvenile: similar to female

Food: aquatic insects, grasses, seeds

Habitat: small ponds, parks, lakes, farms

Sounds: displaying male gives rhythmic huffs during
courtship; female responds with soft quacks

Compare: Usually seen with Domestic Mallards (pg. 87) and
Graylag Geese (pg. 175) in city parks and lakes. The highly variable colors of the Muscovy would make it hard to identify, if not
for the caruncle on its face. Look for the bumpy patch of reddish
skin around the eyes and at the base of the bill.

Stan's Notes: This is the only domestic duck not descended
from the Mallard (pg. 83). Originates from South America, dating
back to the 1400s. Not a cold-weather duck and usually does not
thrive in Minnesota. The wild type, a very dark bird with white
wing patches, is fairly uncommon in North America.

Most Muscovy Ducks were released into suburban ponds, parks
and lakes by the people who raised them, but no longer wanted
to care for them. Others escaped from captivity. They have very
little body fat and usually are raised for their meat, which is lean
and flavorful. *Domestic species—2 pages only*

89

male

female

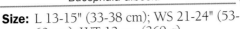

Bufflehead
Bucephala albeola

MIGRATION

Size: L 13-15" (33-38 cm); WS 21-24" (53-60 cm); WT 13 oz. (369 g)

Male: Small duck with striking white sides and a black back. Green purple head with a large bonnet-like white patch. Small gray bill. Non-breeding (Jun-Sep) has light gray sides, a darker gray back and dark head with a less distinct white patch.

Female: overall dark gray to brown with a brown head and small, oval white patch on cheek just behind eyes, small gray bill

Juvenile: similar to female, with a less distinct white patch on cheek

Food: aquatic insects and plants, seeds, snails, mollusks

Habitat: woodland ponds, small lakes, rivers

Sounds: usually silent; courting male gives hoarse cackles and croaks; female responds with loud chattering

Compare: Male Bufflehead shares the white sides and black back with the male Common Goldeneye (pg. 115), but the Goldeneye is larger and lacks the white bonnet-like patch on its head. The male Hooded Merganser (pg. 223) is similar, but larger and lacks the white sides. Look for the green purple head with a large white patch to help identify the male Bufflehead.

The female Bufflehead is commonly confused with the female Common Goldeneye (pg. 115), which is larger and lacks the white cheek patch. The female Lesser Scaup (pg. 103) is also larger and has a white patch at the base of its bill. Look for the white patch on the cheek to help identify the female Bufflehead.

male

Flight: strong direct flight with rapid, shallow wing beats; male has an all-white underside, gray wings with a small white wing patch, pink legs and feet, obvious against the white underside; female is very similar to male, but with less obvious wing patches; head is held higher than the body, feet tuck in during longer flights

flight pattern

Flock: 2-200 individuals; small tight mass in no particular shape or pattern, often flying very high in the sky

Migration: complete migrator, to southern states, Mexico and Central America; few stay in Minnesota on open water in winter

male   female   male

Nesting: cavity, near the water, often in an old woodpecker hole; female lines the cavity with down feathers plucked from her chest and belly; 1 brood

Eggs/Incubation: 8-10 ivory-to-olive eggs; female incubates 29-31 days

Fledging: 50-55 days; female leads young to food; ducklings feed instinctively

Stan's Notes: This bird is the smallest of the diving ducks, with a larger head. The common name refers to the large size of its head and means "buffalo-headed" or "ox-headed."

The Bufflehead is the best diver and one of the most agile diving ducks. Uses its feet only to swim underwater. Frequently dives in groups for safety, with some members of the flock staying on the surface to watch for predators. Like other diving ducks, it takes flight directly from the surface of water without a running start.

Often migrates with other ducks and is seen with other ducks at other times. Nests only in North America.

Female remains with the same mate for many years and is very territorial. Will return to the same nest site annually, freshening the nest every year with new down feathers plucked from her chest. Nests in old woodpecker cavities, but has been known to use a burrow in an earthen bank when tree cavities are scarce. Will also use a nest box. Unlike other ducks, young Buffleheads stay in the nest for up to two days before venturing out with their mother.

male

female

Ruddy Duck
Oxyura jamaicensis

MIGRATION
SUMMER

Size: L 15" (38 cm); WS 18-21" (45-53 cm); WT 1 lb. 2 oz. (.5 kg)

Male: Compact cinnamon body with a large head, black crown and nape. Large bright white cheek patch and distinctive light blue bill. Long, stiff black tail, often raised above water during display. Non-breeding (Sep-Mar) has a dull brown-to-gray body and gray bill.

Female: similar to non-breeding (eclipse) male, with a dark line running across a white cheek, large dark bill and long tail, often raised above water

Juvenile: similar to female, with a less distinct line running across the cheek

Food: aquatic insects and plants, snails

Habitat: ponds, woodland ponds, small lakes, prairie lakes

Sounds: female gives a low nasal call along with a high squeak; male makes unique muffled sounds followed by a staccato "pop" produced by the feet underwater; non-breeding male is silent in fall

Compare: Male Ruddy Duck has a similar size and color as male Cinnamon Teal (pg. 41), but Cinnamon lacks the dark crown, nape and white cheeks. The male Ring-necked Duck (pg. 99) has gray sides and a white ring around its bill. The male Common Goldeneye (pg. 115) has mostly white sides and a green head. The male Hooded Merganser (pg. 223) has a hammerhead crest "hood" with a white patch and long, thin black bill.

Female Ruddy is smaller than the female Common Goldeneye (pg. 115), which has bright yellow eyes and a light gray body. The female Bufflehead (pg. 91) has a plain white cheek patch that lacks a dark horizontal line running through it.

displaying male

Flight: erratic flight, often changing direction, with fast, shallow wing beats; male has a short neck and tail with a gray belly, distinctive dark chest and a large white cheek patch, sometimes seen in flight; female has a gray belly with a brown chest and tail; feet tuck into tail feathers during longer flights

flight pattern

Flock: 2-20 individuals; unorganized mass or straight-line formation, flying low over the water

Migration: complete migrator, to southern states and Mexico

non-breeding male | non-breeding male | females | juvenile

Nesting: ground, very near water in tall vegetation; female builds with green grasses gathered from the immediate area and lines the nest with finer plant material; 1 brood

Eggs/Incubation: 6-8 pale white eggs; female incubates 23-26 days

Fledging: 42-48 days; female and male tend young; ducklings copy feeding behavior of parents

Stan's Notes: A small, compact diver with a unique appearance and color. Legs are set far back on the body, making for awkward walking. Bill is a distinctive light blue, but unlike the Lesser and Greater Scaups (pp. 103-109), the Ruddy is not called Bluebill.

Often secretive, preferring small ponds and lakes with abundant tall vegetation. Flushes quickly when threatened or dives into the water and swims off, staying away for a long time. While diving for food, often resurfaces in the same place. Has the ability to sink slowly under the surface, similar to loons and grebes.

The only duck species to cock its tail out of the water and fan it in display. In late winter and early spring, the courting male performs like a wind-up toy, ratcheting his head quickly up and down, making muffled sounds and finishing with a staccato "pop" made by his feet underwater. Displays to the female with an upright tail, swimming in front of her so she can see the tail fan from behind. Male breeds with more than one female and leaves shortly after incubation starts. A male can be seen with a female and newly hatched ducklings, but this usually is not the father.

The female is a brood parasite, laying some of her eggs in other Ruddy nests. Also lays some eggs in nests of Redheads (pg. 119), Canvasbacks (pg. 123) and grebes (pp. 191-213).

Not seen in large numbers in Minnesota. Once more abundant, its decline is due to lack of habitat and possibly hunting pressures. Usually only seen in pairs during spring and larger groups in fall.

male

female

Ring-necked Duck
Aythya collaris

MIGRATION
SUMMER
WINTER

Size: L 16-17" (40-43 cm); WS 24-28" (60-71 cm); WT 1 lb. 8 oz. (.7 kg)

Male: Striking duck with a black head, chest and back. Gray sides with a white spur near each shoulder. Top of head peaks near the back. Iridescent head shines blue, green or purple, depending on sunlight. Light blue-to-gray bill with a black tip and bold white ring behind the tip and second white ring at the base. Cinnamon ring around the neck, often hidden. Non-breeding (Jul-Sep) is overall brown, lacks gray sides and ring around the bill.

Female: dark brown back, light brown sides, dark brown crown with top of head peaking near the back, gray face with a white eye-ring extending into a line behind each eye, light blue bill with a white ring and black tip

Juvenile: similar to female

Food: aquatic plants and insects, snails

Habitat: ponds, small lakes near or in woodlands

Sounds: usually silent; female gives a harsh quack when disturbed or taking flight; male gives a quiet whirring call that sounds like air blowing through a tube

Compare: Male Ring-necked has a black back unlike the gray back of male Lesser Scaup (pg. 103) and Greater Scaup (pg. 107). The female Ring-necked is very similar to female Lesser Scaup (pg. 103) and Greater Scaup (pg. 107), but both Scaups lack gray cheeks and the white eye-ring.

Check for the white ring around the bill with a black tip to help identify the male and female Ring-necks.

male

Flight: direct flight with rapid, shallow wing beats; male has a white belly, contrasting dark neck and tail and gray wings; female has a white belly, brown neck and tail and gray wings; feet tuck in during longer flights

flight pattern

Flock: 2-200 individuals; small loose mass without formation

Migration: complete migrator, to southern states, Mexico and Central America

female

displaying male

male

Nesting: ground, near the edge of water, sometimes concealed under a shrub; female builds with grasses, mosses and fine plant material gathered from the immediate area and lines the nest with down feathers plucked from her chest and belly; 1 brood

Eggs/Incubation: 8-10 olive gray-to-brown eggs; female incubates 26-27 days

Fledging: 49-56 days; female tends young; ducklings copy feeding behavior of mother

Stan's Notes: Often called Ringbill by duck hunters. One of the most widespread of the duck species, nesting across Minnesota, North Dakota, Wisconsin, Michigan, the Northeast and Canada, and found throughout the lower half of the U.S. in winter. Usually seen in smaller, shallow freshwater lakes during summer. During winter it prefers freshwater ponds as opposed to some ducks that switch to brackish water or salt water.

A diving duck, watch for it to compress its feathers together to expel trapped air before diving underwater to forage for food. Can dive as deep as 40 feet (12 m) in search of something to eat. Takes to flight by quickly springing up off water, but more often swims away rapidly when threatened.

A monogamous breeder and solitary nester. Young leave the nest within 24 hours of hatching and feed instinctively on their own while being tended by their mother.

Named "Ring-necked" because of its cinnamon collar, but this is nearly impossible to see in the field unless the duck is alert and raising its head. Also known as Ring-billed Duck due to the white ring around its bill.

male

female

Lesser Scaup
Aythya affinis

MIGRATION
SUMMER
WINTER

Size: L 16-17" (40-43 cm); WS 25-29" (63-74 cm); WT 1 lb. 14 oz. (.8 kg)

Male: Appears mostly black with bold white sides and a gray back. Nearly black head, slightly pointed in back and appearing green or purple in direct sun. Large blue bill with a tiny black tip (nail). Nearly black chest. Black rump and tail. Bright yellow eyes. Non-breeding (Jul-Oct) is overall brown and lacks the white sides and green head.

Female: overall brown, back of head is higher than front, light blue bill with a tiny black nail and white patch at the base, yellow eyes

Juvenile: similar to female, with a flatter head

Food: aquatic plants and insects

Habitat: small lakes, prairie pothole lakes, ponds, marshes

Sounds: female gives a repetitious rough, grating call that sounds like purring; courting male gives a low single-note whistle

Compare: Male Lesser Scaup is slightly smaller than male Greater Scaup (pg. 107), which has a more rounded head rather than a pointed back of head. Male Common Goldeneye (pg. 115) has a white patch on each side of its face and a white chest. The male Ring-necked Duck (pg. 99) has gray sides and a bold white ring around its bill near the tip.

Female Lesser Scaup is nearly identical to female Greater Scaup (pg. 107), but Greater Scaup has a more rounded head. Female Ring-necked Duck (pg. 99) is very similar, but it has a gray face, white ring around its bill near the tip and dark eyes. The female Canvasback (pg. 123) has a sloping forehead and long dark bill.

103

male

Flight: fast direct flight with rapid wing beats; male has a distinctive white belly and underwings that contrast with a dark chest, neck and tail; female has a whitewashed brown belly, gray wing linings and dark chest, neck and tail; feet tuck in during longer flights

flight pattern

Flock: 2-200 individuals; unorganized formation with no apparent leader

Migration: complete migrator, to southern states, Mexico and Central America

male   juvenile   male   non-breeding male

Nesting: ground, within 150 feet (46 m) of water's edge; female builds with a small amount of vegetation gathered from the immediate area and sparsely lines the nest with down feathers plucked from her chest and belly; 1 brood

Eggs/Incubation: 8-14 olive buff eggs; female incubates 22-28 days

Fledging: 45-50 days; female tends young; ducklings copy feeding behavior of mother

Stan's Notes: Often called Bluebill. One of the most abundant diving ducks in North America. Not too common in Minnesota, but more so than the Greater Scaup (pg. 107). Usually found on small lakes and prairie pothole lakes. Often in large flocks of up to several thousand birds during migration and winter.

Dives to feed on the bottom of lakes unlike dabbling ducks, which only tip forward to reach bottom. Like other waterfowl, it suffers from acute lead poisoning, resulting in death, after it feeds on the lake bottom and ingests lead shot.

Many people think a good way to distinguish between Lesser and Greater Scaups is to look at the head color of the male. This is not a reliable method since the head of both species can appear green or purplish blue in direct sunlight.

A monogamous duck, with mates staying together possibly for several seasons. Unlike the Greater Scaup, the Lesser is a solitary nester and builds its nest farther from the water's edge than the Greater. Male leaves the female when she starts to incubate eggs. Quantity of eggs (clutch size) increases with the age of the female.

The mother leads ducklings to water shortly after they hatch, where they watch her feed and copy the behavior. Ducklings gather together in groups (crèches) for baby-sitting by 1-3 adult females while the mothers are away feeding. Young Lesser Scaups start to fly at 45-50 days of age.

male

female

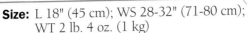

Greater Scaup
Aythya marila

MIGRATION
WINTER

Size: L 18" (45 cm); WS 28-32" (71-80 cm);
WT 2 lb. 4 oz. (1 kg)

Male: Mostly black and white with bright white sides and a gray back. Rounded black head, appearing green or bluish in direct sun. Light blue bill with a black tip (nail). Black rump and tail. Yellow eyes. Non-breeding (Jul-Sep) is overall gray with a dark head, neck and chest.

Female: overall brown with a darker head that is rounded at the top, blue bill with a dark nail and bold white patch at the base, may have a white patch behind each eye

Juvenile: similar to female, with a sloped top of head

Food: aquatic plants in summer, mollusks and aquatic insects in winter

Habitat: ponds, small lakes near woodlands, prairie lakes

Sounds: female gives a repetitious rough or hoarse call; male is often silent, sometimes gives a soft hoot

Compare: Male Greater Scaup is very similar to male Lesser Scaup (pg. 103), but the Greater is slightly larger and has a more rounded head and larger black nail. Male Common Goldeneye (pg. 115) has a white chest and distinctive white mark in front of each eye. Male Ring-necked Duck (pg. 99) has a bold white ring around its bill, black back and slightly smaller size.

Female Greater Scaup is very similar to the female Lesser Scaup (pg. 103), but the Lesser has a more pointed head. The female Canvasback (pg. 123) has a larger size, sloping forehead and long dark bill.

group

Flight: fast direct flight with rapid wing beats; male has a distinctive white belly and underwings that contrast with a dark chest, neck and tail; female has a whitewashed brown belly, gray wing linings and dark chest, neck and tail; feet tuck in during longer flights

flight pattern

Flock: 2–200 individuals; unorganized formation with no apparent leader

Migration: complete migrator, to the Pacific, Atlantic and Gulf coasts and Mexico

male

Nesting: ground, near the edge of water; female builds with plants gathered from the immediate area and lines the nest with down feathers plucked from her chest and belly; 1 brood

Eggs/Incubation: 7-10 greenish olive eggs; female incubates 24-28 days

Fledging: 45-50 days; female tends young; ducklings copy feeding behavior of mother

Stan's Notes: Frequently called Bluebill by hunters. A migrant in Minnesota, breeding in the southern two-thirds of Alaska and northern Canada. Spends the summer on freshwater ponds and lakes and winters primarily in salt water or brackish water. During winter it can be seen in extremely large flocks of tens of thousands of birds, but this is not common in Minnesota. More common than the Lesser Scaup (pg. 103) before 1920; now Lesser Scaup is more common.

This is a large diving duck, diving down as far as 20 feet (6 m) to find food–aquatic plants in summer and various aquatic insects and mollusks in winter. At a distance, it appears to be black and white. Closer up, the head of the male usually looks greenish, but may appear bluish depending on available sunlight and the angle of observation. Its gray back has fine grayish barring that is often hard to see; however, comparing it with the medium barring on the back of a Lesser Scaup can help differentiate the two species.

Monogamous, remaining with the same mate for several seasons. May nest in small colonies mixed with Lesser Scaups.

An adult female will sometimes lay her eggs in the nest of another female, which results in some mothers incubating clutches of 11 or more eggs. Female performs all incubation and leads ducklings to water shortly after hatching. Ducklings learn to find their own food by watching their mother's feeding behavior. Female Greater Scaups may cooperatively defend and care for young.

male

female

Barrow's Goldeneye
Bucephala islandica

RARE

Size: L 18-20" (45-50 cm); WS 26-30" (66-76 cm); WT 2 lb. 1 oz. (.9 kg)

Male: Black and white duck. Large puffy head, low and flat on top, appearing deep green or purplish in bright sun. Bright golden eyes. Large crescent-shaped white mark on each side of face in front of the eyes. Black spur near each shoulder. Small dark bill. Non-breeding (Aug-Nov) is overall gray with a darker head and white ring around neck.

Female: overall gray body, large dark brown head, bright golden eyes, white collar (often hidden), small yellow bill

Juvenile: same as female, but has a dark bill

Food: aquatic insects and plants, crayfish, mollusks

Habitat: small ponds with dense vegetation, small lakes

Sounds: female gives a low hoarse quack; male gives a weak grunting call; wings produce a high-pitched whistling sound during flight

Compare: Barrow's Goldeneye is very uncommon in Minnesota. Male Common Goldeneye (pg. 115) has a round white spot on each side of its face in front of the eyes and a tall, almost peaked top of head. Male Bufflehead (pg. 91) shares the white sides and black back, but it has a white bonnet-like patch on the head. Look for the white chest, white crescent mark on each side of the face and golden eyes to help identify the male Barrow's.

Female Barrow's is nearly identical to female Common Goldeneye (pg. 115), but Common Goldeneye has a dark bill with a yellow tip. Female Lesser Scaup (pg. 103) has a white patch at the base of its bill. Female Bufflehead (pg. 91) is smaller, with a small white patch on each cheek behind the eyes and a gray bill.

111

male

Flight: fast direct flight with rapid, shallow wing beats; male has an all-white underside with dark underwings, white wing patches and a dark head and tail; male has more white on its underside than do most other waterfowl; female has a gray chest, white belly and dark head; feet tuck in during longer flights

flight pattern

Flock: 2-200 individuals; small tight flock in no particular shape or pattern, often flying very high in the sky

Migration: complete migrator, to the Atlantic and Pacific coasts; very small percentage remain in Minnesota during winter

males

male small group

female

Nesting: cavity, near the water in a tree cavity, old woodpecker hole or wooden box; female fills cavity with wood chips and lines it with down feathers plucked from her chest and belly; 1 brood

Eggs/Incubation: 9-11 green-to-olive eggs; female incubates 32-34 days

Fledging: 55-60 days; female leads young to food; ducklings feed instinctively

Stan's Notes: Very uncommon in Minnesota. The Barrow's nests in Alaska and northwestern Canada and usually winters along the Pacific coast and at some inland sites. This is unlike the closely related Common Goldeneye (pg. 115), which is found throughout Minnesota during migration and in the northern half of the state during summer.

Barrow's has a strong attraction to its breeding and wintering sites alike and will return to the same ponds each season. A few birds, often males, show up in Minnesota during winter and are usually seen with Common Goldeneyes or other duck species.

Often swims out to open water when threatened instead of flying away. Able to dive and remain underwater for up to one minute.

The female frequently returns to the same nest location for many years and may mate with the same male from year to year. Like the Common Goldeneye, Barrow's uses a nest box when available. Hybridizes with the Common Goldeneye, producing birds with a maroon head.

Pair bonds may last for several seasons, but once the female starts incubating, the male leaves and does not help her raise the young. Female will "adopt" orphaned goldeneye ducklings. Young leave the nest 24-36 hours after hatching and begin to fly when they reach 55-60 days of age.

male

female

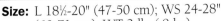

Common Goldeneye
Bucephala clangula

MIGRATION
SUMMER
WINTER

Size: L 18½-20" (47-50 cm); WS 24-28" (60-71 cm); WT 2 lb. (.9 kg)

Male: A mostly white duck with a black back and large, puffy green head that appears tall and peaked at the forehead. Bright golden eyes. Large white spot on each side of face in front of eyes. Small dark bill. Non-breeding (Aug-Nov) is overall gray with a darker head and white ring around neck.

Female: overall gray body, large dark brown head, bright golden eyes, white collar (often hidden), dark bill with a yellow tip

Juvenile: same as female, but lacks the yellow tip on bill

Food: aquatic insects and plants, crayfish, mollusks

Habitat: ponds, small to large lakes, rivers

Sounds: female gives hoarse quacks when agitated; courting male gives a single raspy nasal call; wings produce a high-pitched whistling sound in flight

Compare: Male Common Goldeneye is very similar to Barrow's Goldeneye (pg. 111), but Barrow's has a white crescent on each side of its face. Male Lesser Scaup (pg. 103) and Greater Scaup (pg. 107) both have a gray back and larger, light blue bill. Male Bufflehead (pg. 91) is smaller, with a white bonnet-like patch on its head. Look for the white chest, round white spot on each side of the face and golden eyes to identify male Common Goldeneye.

Female Common Goldeneye is nearly identical to female Barrow's Goldeneye (pg. 111), but Barrow's has a yellow bill. Female Lesser Scaup (pg. 103) has a white patch at the base of its bill. Female Bufflehead (pg. 91) is smaller, with a small white patch behind its eyes and a gray bill. Female Redhead (pg. 119) is similar in size, but lacks the gray body of female Common Goldeneye.

threat alert

Flight: fast direct flight with rapid, shallow wing beats; male has an all-white underside with dark underwings, white wing patches and a dark head and tail; male has more white on its underside than do most other waterfowl; female has a gray chest, white belly and dark head; feet tuck in during longer flights

flight pattern

Flock: 2-200 individuals; small tight mass in no particular shape or pattern, often flying very high in the sky

Migration: complete migrator, to southern states and Mexico; some remain in parts of Minnesota on open water during winter

displaying male   diving female   small group

Nesting: cavity, near the water in a tree cavity, old woodpecker hole or wooden box; female fills cavity with wood chips and lines it with down feathers plucked from her chest and belly; 1 brood

Eggs/Incubation: 8-10 light green eggs; female incubates 28-32 days

Fledging: 56-59 days; female leads young to food; ducklings feed instinctively

Stan's Notes: Received the common name "Goldeneye" from its obvious bright golden eyes. A common duck of shallow woodland ponds and small lakes. Known for the loud whistling sound its wings produce during flight.

One of the few duck species that uses a cavity for nesting, often a natural cavity in a tree. Will take an old woodpecker hole and accepts a wooden nest box in a tree or on a pole.

Doesn't breed until the second year. During late winter and early spring, male attracts a female with an elaborate display, throwing his head backward to his rump while uttering a single raspy note.

When competition for nest sites is too high or there is a lack of nest cavities, mated females sometimes lay their eggs in the nests of other goldeneyes, which results in some females incubating up to 30 eggs. In nests with many eggs, some eggs near the bottom don't get warm enough and will not hatch. Unmated females and females that have lost their eggs or brood will look for other nest cavities, but mated females won't breed again during that season.

Ducklings stay in the nest cavity for up to 48 hours before leaving, when they follow their mother to the water. Female tends young, but they feed themselves instinctively. Male does not help her raise the young. Ducklings grow quickly and take their first flight between 55-60 days of age.

male

female

Redhead
Aythya americana

MIGRATION
SUMMER

Size: L 19¼" (49 cm); WS 29-32" (74-80 cm);
WT 2 lb. 4 oz. (1 kg)

Male: Large, rounded red head with a red neck. Black
chest and tail. Smoky gray sides, wings and back.
Tricolored bill with a light blue base, white ring
and black tip. Non-breeding (Jul-Sep) is overall
brown to gray with a dull red head and gray bill
with a black tip.

Female: plain, soft brown duck, sometimes with an overall gray wash, large round head, gray bill with a
black tip

Juvenile: similar to female

Food: seeds, aquatic plants and insects, crustaceans,
snails

Habitat: small to large lakes, prairie pothole lakes

Sounds: female gives a harsh squawk; courting male gives
a cat-like mewing that is sometimes followed by
a trilling call

Compare: Male Redhead is smaller than the male Canvasback
(pg. 123), which has a larger, darker head, long sloping forehead
and large black bill. Male Northern Shoveler (pg. 67) has a green
head and rusty red sides unlike the red head and gray sides of the
male Redhead.

Female Redhead is smaller than female Canvasback (pg. 123),
which has a thicker neck, larger head and long dark bill. Female
Northern Shoveler (pg. 67) is lighter brown than female Redhead
and has an exceptionally large spoon-shaped bill.

119

male

Flight: fast direct flight with strong wing beats; male has a bold white belly, contrasting black neck and tail and white-to-gray wing linings; female has a gray belly, tan neck and tail and white-to-gray wing linings; feet tuck in during longer flights

flight pattern

Flock: 2-200 individuals; large V or irregularly shaped flock that flies low or high over the water

Migration: complete migrator, to southern states, southwestern states, Mexico and Central America

male   female   pair   juvenile

Nesting: cup, in shallow water on a mat of floating vegetation; female builds with dead aquatic plants gathered from the immediate area and lines the nest with finer plant material and down feathers plucked from her chest and belly; 1 brood

Eggs/Incubation: 9-14 pale white eggs; female and male incubate 24-28 days

Fledging: 56-73 days; female leads young to food; ducklings feed instinctively

Stan's Notes: A diving duck of permanent large bodies of water. Forages along the shoreline in the morning and evening, feeding on seeds and aquatic plants and insects. Often seen in large flocks when resting (rafting) and in small groups in shallow water when it feeds.

During flight, it appears as though it is always in a hurry to get somewhere. Flock usually flies in a V shape during migration and in irregular formation when flying to and from feeding areas.

A monogamous breeder. Usually builds nest on the surface of the water, using a large mat of vegetation. Nests near other Redhead nesters. Female lays up to 75 percent of her eggs in the nests of other Redheads and several other duck species such as the Canvasback (pg. 123). Some females have no nests of their own, laying 100 percent of their eggs in the nests of other ducks.

A freshwater nester in the Prairie Pothole region of the northern Great Plains. More common in western states during spring and summer. Some migrate east in the fall, spending the winter in the eastern U.S., often on marine (saltwater) bays.

male

female

MIGRATION
SUMMER
WINTER

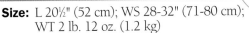

Canvasback
Aythya valisineria

Size: L 20½" (52 cm); WS 28-32" (71-80 cm);
WT 2 lb. 12 oz. (1.2 kg)

Male: Large head with a sloping forehead, transitioning into a long black bill. Head is deep red to almost brown, with a red neck. Sides and back are gray to nearly white. Black chest, rump and tail. Non-breeding (Jul-Sep) is similar, with a tan body.

Female: similar shape as male, with a brown head, neck and chest, light gray-to-brown sides and long dark bill

Juvenile: similar to female

Food: aquatic plants and insects, small clams

Habitat: lakes, rivers, ponds

Sounds: female gives a low growling call or quack; courting male gives a soft cooing call when displaying or during aerial chases

Compare: The male Canvasback is larger than the male Greater Scaup (pg. 107) and Lesser Scaup (pg. 103), both of which lack the red head and neck and have shorter, light blue bills. Larger than the male Redhead (pg. 119), which has gray sides and a smaller, tricolored bill with a light blue base, white ring and black tip.

Female Canvasback has a larger size than female Greater Scaup (pg. 107) and Lesser Scaup (pg. 103), but the Scaups have a white patch at base of their bills and lack a sloping forehead and long dark bill. The female Redhead (pg. 119) has a rounded head, is overall browner and lacks the sloping forehead of a Canvasback.

male

Flight: strong direct flight with rapid wing beats; male has a bright white belly and wing linings with a dark chest, neck, tail and head; female has a bright white belly and wing linings with a brown chest, neck, tail and head; feet tuck in during longer flights

flight pattern

Flock: 20-200 individuals; irregularly shaped flock, small V or short straight-line formation

Migration: complete migrator, to southern states, the Atlantic, Pacific and Gulf coasts and Mexico

female   male

Nesting: ground, in shallow water up to 2 feet (.6 m) deep, well concealed by vegetation, occasionally atop a muskrat lodge; female builds with reeds and grasses gathered from the immediate area and lines the nest with finer plants and down feathers plucked from her chest and belly; 1 brood

Eggs/Incubation: 7-9 pale white-to-gray eggs; female incubates 24-29 days

Fledging: 56-67 days; female leads young to food; ducklings feed instinctively

Stan's Notes: One of the largest and heaviest ducks in North America. A large diving duck of larger freshwater lakes, rivers and ponds. Flies very high and is wary of people, moving out to open water when there is any disturbance on shore.

Mates during migration or on the breeding grounds. The females return to their birthplace (philopatric), taking a new mate every year, while the males disperse to new areas. A courting male will softly coo during display and aerial chases. Male leaves the female after incubation starts. Female feeds very little during incubation and loses up to 70 percent of fat reserves at that time.

Hybridizes with Redheads (pg. 119), with female Redheads later laying their eggs in the nests of Canvasbacks (nest parasitism). Populations declined dramatically in the 1960-80s due to marsh drainage for agriculture, drought and various other reasons.

male

female

Harlequin Duck
Histrionicus histrionicus

WINTER

Size: L 17" (43 cm); WS 24-28" (60-71 cm);
WT 1 lb. 4 oz. (.6 kg)

Male: Unique black and white pattern with rusty red
sides and top of head. Highest part of head is just
above eyes. Small light-colored bill. Long pointed
tail. Non-breeding (Jul-Sep) is overall brown with
a white patch on the sides of head and at the base
of bill, and faint white marks at the shoulders and
base of tail.

Female: overall brown duck with a white patch on the
sides of head, small short bill with a white patch
at the base and long, pointed dark tail

Juvenile: similar to female

Food: aquatic insects, crustaceans, mollusks

Habitat: fast-running streams and rivers in open tundra
in spring and summer, coastal waters and large
freshwater lakes during migration and winter

Sounds: usually silent; courting male gives high-pitched
squeaks; female responds with nasal quacking

Compare: Male Harlequin is similar in size to the male Greater
Scaup (pg. 107) and Lesser Scaup (pg. 103), but the Scaups have
white sides. The male Long-tailed Duck (pg. 131) has gray sides
and an extremely long tail. Look for the distinctive black and
white pattern combined with rust sides to help identify the male
Harlequin Duck.

Female Harlequin is the same size as female Long-tailed Duck
(pg. 131), but the Long-tailed has white around its eyes and a
large white rump. Female Bufflehead (pg. 91) is smaller and lacks
a white patch at the base of its bill.

male

Flight: fast direct flight with strong wing beats; male is overall dark with a lighter belly, 2 white bars on the chest and neck, and dark wings; female is overall dark with a white belly and dark wing linings; feet tuck in during longer flights

flight pattern

Flock: 2-20 individuals; small compact flock with no particular pattern, flying low over the water, often turning abruptly

Migration: partial to non-migrator, to the Alaskan, Canadian and Atlantic coasts

male
female
male small group

Nesting: ground, within 100 feet (30 m) of the edge of water, often under a shrub; female builds with dried grasses gathered from the immediate area and lines nest with finer plant material and down feathers plucked from her chest and belly; 1 brood

Eggs/Incubation: 6-8 pale white eggs; female incubates 28-31 days

Fledging: 60-70 days; female leads young to food; ducklings feed instinctively

Stan's Notes: A small duck that rides low in water. Usually seen along rocky seacoasts in winter, but can be found on large freshwater lakes during migration and winter. Found during breeding season and summer in fast-running rivers and streams, which are presumed to have a richer food supply than slow-moving waters. Most common along the Alaskan and Canadian coasts, but also seen on the Atlantic coast, to a lesser extent.

The name "Harlequin" refers to the diamond shapes and patterns on the male. Also known as Torrent Duck because it frequently walks in very fast or turbulent shallow water with its head down, foraging for food among the rocks on the bottom. When diving in deeper water, it uses its wings and feet to propel itself underwater unlike other diving ducks, which just use their feet.

A monogamous breeder and solitary nester. Female does not start to breed until she reaches 2 years of age. Male leaves the female after she begins to incubate. Ducklings leave the nest shortly after they hatch and take their first flight at 40-45 days of age.

male

female

WINTER

Long-tailed Duck
Clangula hyemalis

Size: L 17" (43 cm); WS 26-30" (66-76 cm); WT 1 lb. 10 oz. (.7 kg)

Male: Uniquely shaped and patterned duck with a black head and neck and whitish gray face. Gray sides. Dark back and brown wings. Small dark bill with a tan ring near the tip. A very long, narrow tail. Non-breeding (Nov-Apr) has a white head and neck, black and gray patches on face and long tail.

Female: overall brown duck with a dark face, white at the base of neck and around the eyes, small dark bill, large white rump and short tail; non-breeding has a white face and sides

Juvenile: similar to non-breeding female

Food: aquatic insects and plants, mollusks, crustaceans

Habitat: shallow freshwater lakes during breeding season, coastal waters and large freshwater lakes during migration and early winter

Sounds: male gives a melodious yodeling call; female gives soft calls and grunts; very vocal from late winter to early spring

Compare: Male Long-tailed is the same size as male Harlequin Duck (pg. 127), but Harlequin has rusty red sides and a shorter tail. Look for the extremely long tail, whitish gray face and black head to help identify the male Long-tailed Duck.

Female Long-tailed is the same size as the female Harlequin Duck (pg. 127), which lacks the white rump and white mark at the base of neck.

non-breeding male

Flight: very fast flight with fast, shallow wing beats and erratic side-to-side turns of the body that show the belly; male has a black chest, neck and head that contrast sharply with a white belly and rump, an extremely long, thin dark tail and dark wing linings; female is very similar to male, with a shorter tail; feet tuck in during longer flights

flight pattern

Flock: 2-20 individuals; small tight flock that flies very close to the water's surface

Migration: complete migrator, to coastal Alaska and Canada and large freshwater lakes

non-breeding male

non-breeding female

non-breeding male

non-breeding small group

Nesting: ground, near the edge of water, concealed in vegetation; female neatly builds with mosses, sedges and grasses gathered from the immediate area and lines the nest with leaves and down feathers plucked from her chest and belly; 1 brood

Eggs/Incubation: 6-8 pale green eggs; female incubates 24-29 days

Fledging: 35-40 days; female leads young to food; ducklings feed instinctively

Stan's Notes: A gregarious sea duck. Usually seen in Alaska and northern parts of Canada during summer. Gathers in extremely large flocks in some areas along the Atlantic and Pacific coasts in winter. Large numbers of birds often get caught in fishing nets, with many killed as a result. A few individuals can be found on Lake Superior during migration, when it moves from the north to the coasts.

Unlike most other ducks, the Long-tailed is very vocal. Formerly called Oldsquaw, a reference to its almost continuous chatter. The male has a yodeling call instead of a quack, while the female gives soft calls and grunts.

The Long-tailed has a very unusual molting pattern. Molts almost continuously except for the male's tail, which is always long and easily visible in flight. A fast flyer, flying in small groups just above the surface of water, making characteristic turns of the body from side to side.

One of the deepest diving ducks, diving down to 200 feet (61 m). Can stay submerged for up to a minute and a half.

After hatching, ducklings form groups (crèches) that frequently consist of 10-30 individuals (3-4 broods), but may have as many as 100 individuals. Older females often tend the crèches.

male

female

Black Scoter
Melanitta nigra

MIGRATION

Size: L 19½" (49.5 cm); WS 30-32" (76-80 cm); WT 2 lb. 1 oz. (.9 kg)

Male: All-black duck with a large yellow knob at base of bill. Bulbous head appears large for the body. Black legs and feet. Narrow pointed tail.

Female: all brown with a dark crown, pale white cheeks, thin dark bill and long thin tail

Juvenile: similar to female

Food: mollusks, crustaceans, aquatic plants, seeds

Habitat: tundra lakes, small to large lakes, ponds, rivers, Lake Superior during migration

Sounds: female gives a low hoarse grunt; male makes a slurred, high-pitched (piping) sound along with a plaintive whistle; wings produce a whistling sound during flight

Compare: Male Black Scoter is smaller than male White-winged Scoter (pg. 143), which has a small comma-shaped white mark beneath each eye and an orange and yellow bill. The male Surf Scoter (pg. 139) is slightly larger and has a white patch on its forehead, another longer white patch on the nape of neck and a large multicolored bill.

Female Black Scoter is smaller than female White-winged Scoter (pg. 143), which has a white patch at the base of its bill, another white patch in back of its eyes and a larger bill. The female Surf Scoter (pg. 139) is slightly larger, with a vertical white patch at the base of its bill and white mark on the nape.

male

Flight: strong direct flight with rapid wing beats; male has an all-black underside and wings with dark gray trailing edges; female has a lighter belly than male and white cheeks; juvenile has a white belly and chin and dark wings; feet tuck in during longer flights

flight pattern

Flock: 2-20 individuals; straight-line or V-shaped formation

Migration: complete migrator, to the Atlantic and Pacific coasts, Gulf of Mexico and Mexico; in Minnesota only during migration on large bodies of water such as Lake Superior

displaying male   female   flock   male small group

Nesting: ground, near the water's edge; female builds with plants gathered from the immediate area and lines the nest with finer vegetation and down feathers plucked from her chest and belly; 1 brood

Eggs/Incubation: 6-8 light pink-to-buff eggs; female incubates 30-31 days

Fledging: 45-50 days; female tends young; ducklings copy feeding behavior of mother

Stan's Notes: The least common of the scoters, although it once was known as the Common Scoter. Found in Minnesota on Lake Superior during migration, but also seen throughout the state on larger lakes and rivers. Frequently in mixed flocks of hundreds of ducks or in small groups of same sex birds. Nests on tundra near freshwater lakes and ponds, returning to the Atlantic and Pacific coasts for the remainder of the summer and winter, with males often wintering farther north at sea than the females.

A diving sea duck, usually feeding in water 20-40 feet (6-12 m) deep, just outside the breaker zone. Rides low in the water, with less than half of its body showing above the surface.

The male is the only all-black duck in North America that has black legs and feet. Grayish feathers on wings, seen only in flight, contrast with its black wing linings and help identify this species in flight.

Female doesn't breed until her third summer. Male leaves female shortly after she starts to incubate. Broods sometimes gather into groups called crèches for baby-sitting by 1-3 older females.

male

female

Surf Scoter
Melanitta perspicillata

MIGRATION

Size: L 20" (50 cm); WS 30-34" (76-86 cm); WT 2 lb. 1 oz. (.9 kg)

Male: Black duck with a white patch on the forehead and long white patch on the nape of neck. Bright white eyes. Large multicolored bill with a white base, black spot on each side of the base and an orange tip (nail).

Female: brown duck with a darker brown crown, white mark on the nape and dark bill with a vertical white patch at the base

Juvenile: similar to female

Food: mollusks, crustaceans, aquatic insects, fish eggs

Habitat: small ponds, bogs, slow-moving streams near forests, large lakes such as Lake Superior during migration

Sounds: usually very quiet; female occasionally makes a croaking sound; male gives a low clear whistle or makes a gurgling sound, like bubbling liquid; wings of male produce a low whistle

Compare: Male Surf Scoter is slightly larger than the male Black Scoter (pg. 135), which has a large yellow knob on its bill and lacks the white patches on its head and nape. The male White-winged Scoter (pg. 143) is slightly larger, with a comma-shaped white mark beneath its eyes and a smaller orange and yellow bill.

Female Surf Scoter is slightly larger than the female Black Scoter (pg. 135), which has pale white cheeks and a much smaller bill. Female White-winged Scoter (pg. 143) is slightly larger and lacks the white patch on the nape of its neck.

juvenile male

Flight: strong direct flight with rapid wing beats; male has an all-black underside and wings with dark gray trailing edges; female has a lighter belly than male; juvenile has a white belly and dark wing linings; feet tuck in during longer flights

flight pattern

Flock: 2-20 individuals; straight-line formation

Migration: complete migrator, to the Atlantic and Pacific coasts, Gulf of Mexico and Mexico

male

Nesting: ground, often far from the water, in a cluster of small spruce or dwarf willow trees or on a grass tussock; female builds with dried vegetation gathered from the immediate area and lines the nest with down feathers from her chest and belly; 1 brood

Eggs/Incubation: 5-8 light pink-to-buff eggs; female incubates 30-31 days

Fledging: 45-50 days; female tends young; ducklings copy feeding behavior of mother

Stan's Notes: A diving sea duck that dives or scoots through the breaking surf, giving rise to the first part of its common name. "Scoter," however, may have originated from its sooty plumage, referring to the black color. Also called Skunkhead for the black and white pattern on the head of the male. Its sloping forehead transitions into a large bill, similar to that of Canvasback (pg. 123).

Fish eggs make up 90 percent of the diet during spring and early summer. Dives as far as 40 feet (12 m) to forage for mussels and crustaceans.

A monogamous breeder. Male leaves shortly after female starts to incubate. Young leave the nest within hours after hatching and take their first flight at 50-55 days of age.

Often seen flying in long strings only during migration, when it moves from one location to another. Nests on tundra throughout Canada and Alaska near freshwater lakes and ponds. Returns to the sea for winter, rarely returning to shore after nesting is complete. Sometimes mixes in flocks with other scoters on the Atlantic and Pacific coasts, where flocks of hundreds of individuals gather during winter.

male

female

White-winged Scoter
Melanitta fusca

MIGRATION

Size: L 20½" (52 cm); WS 33-35" (84-88 cm); WT 3 lb. 12 oz. (1.7 kg)

Male: Black duck with a white patch on trailing edge of wings and comma-shaped white mark beneath eyes. Bright white eyes. Long, thin orange and yellow bill with a small knob at the base. Short thick neck.

Female: overall dark brown with a dark crown, dull white patch just behind eyes and long, narrow dark bill with a dull white patch at the base

Juvenile: similar to female, lighter brown and with more white behind the eyes and at the base of bill

Food: mollusks, crustaceans, aquatic insects and plants

Habitat: ponds, prairie pothole lakes, lakes, slow-moving streams, on Lake Superior during migration

Sounds: usually silent; both sexes may give a harsh croak or quack; wings of male produce a whistle during flight displays

Compare: The male White-winged Scoter is larger than the male Black Scoter (pg. 135), which has a large yellow knob at the base of its bill and lacks the white mark near each eye. The male Surf Scoter (pg. 139) is slightly smaller, with a large multicolored bill and white patches on its forehead and nape.

The female White-winged Scoter is larger than the female Black Scoter (pg. 135), which has pale white cheeks and a smaller bill. Female Surf Scoter (pg. 139) is slightly smaller and has a vertical white patch at the base of its bill and another white patch on the nape of neck.

male

Flight: very fast, direct flight with strong, steady wing beats; male has a dark belly, neck and head, white wing patch on trailing edges and orange feet; female and juvenile look very similar to male; feet extend beyond the tail

flight pattern

Flock: 2-200 individuals; bunched, straight-line or V formation, often flying just above the water's surface

Migration: complete migrator, to the Atlantic and Pacific coasts and Mexico

Nesting: ground, as far as 350 feet (107 m) from water, hidden under a shrub; female builds with plant material gathered from the immediate area and lines the nest with down feathers plucked from her chest and belly; 1 brood

Eggs/Incubation: 5-10 light pink-to-buff eggs; female incubates 28-31 days

Fledging: 50-60 days; female tends young; ducklings copy feeding behavior of mother

Stan's Notes: This is the largest of scoters and perhaps the most common and abundant, sometimes found in mixed flocks with other scoter species. A diving sea duck, seen on Lake Superior during migration. Migrates to the Atlantic and Pacific coasts and goes out to sea for the winter, rarely returning to shore.

Dives to depths of 40 feet (12 m) to feed on shellfish, which it swallows whole. Small stones stored in its large powerful gizzard break up food and aid digestion.

Nests on tundra throughout Alaska and Canada near freshwater lakes and ponds. A monogamous breeder and solitary nester. Ducklings leave nest shortly after hatching and are tended only by the female. Young take their first flight at 65-75 days of age.

The genus name *Melanitta* from the Greek *melas* for "black" and *netta* for "duck" describes this bird well. Common name "White-winged," first used in the *Collective Catalogue of Birds* (1674), refers to the white wing patch (speculum)–although this is sometimes not visible when the bird is resting on the water's surface. The White-winged is the only scoter with a white speculum.

male

female

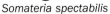

King Eider
Somateria spectabilis

RARE

Size: L 20-24" (50-60 cm); WS 35-38" (88-96 cm); WT 3 lb. 12 oz. (1.7 kg)

Male: Large-bodied black and white duck with a small blue-gray head and short neck. Greenish wash to the cheeks. Small red-to-orange bill with a large yellow-to-orange knob outlined in black from the base of bill to forehead. Non-breeding (Jul-Nov) is overall brown with a yellow bill and knob.

Female: overall brown with a short thick neck, faint tan eye line arching down head and neck, long dark bill

Juvenile: male is similar to non-breeding (eclipse) adult male, lacks the yellow knob at base of bill; female is similar to adult female

Food: mollusks, crustaceans, aquatic insects and plants

Habitat: large lakes during migration and winter, ponds and pools during the breeding season

Sounds: female gives a low quack and makes a croaking sound; courting male gives a low dove-like coo

Compare: The King Eider is not common in Minnesota. The male Eider is slightly larger than the male Surf Scoter (pg. 139), which lacks the light chest and blue-gray head. Look for the prominent yellow-to-orange knob at the base of the bill to help identify the male Eider.

Female King Eider has a similar size as the female Canvasback (pg. 123), but Canvasback has a larger bill and sloped forehead. Because of the rarity of Eiders in Minnesota, much more careful identification of the plain female is needed than for the colorful, distinctive male. Look for the faint eye line extending down the head and neck to help distinguish the female King Eider from other brown ducks.

female

Flight: slow direct flight with rapid wing beats, seen flying low over water; male has a black body and white neck, head and wing linings with a distinctive white patch on the upper surface of wings; female is brown with some white on wing linings; feet tuck in during longer flights

flight pattern

Flock: 2-20 individuals; side by side in a straight line, flying low over the water

Migration: complete migrator, to the Atlantic and Pacific coasts; seen on the Great Lakes during migration and early winter

Nesting: ground, within 50 feet (15 m) of the water's edge; female builds with vegetation gathered from the immediate area and lines the nest with down feathers from her chest and belly; 1 brood

Eggs/Incubation: 4-5 olive eggs; female incubates 22-24 days

Fledging: 40-50 days; female leads young to food; ducklings feed instinctively

Stan's Notes: This duck occurs only occasionally in Minnesota. Most are seen in small flocks on Lake Mille Lacs, Lower Red Lake and other larger lakes during migration and on Lake Superior in winter. Individuals may join flocks of other duck species, but the Eider generally does not mix with other flocks. Usually found in large flocks in places other than Minnesota.

Considered a sea duck (pelagic), normally spending the winter at sea off the coasts of Alaska and Canada. Prefers rocky shores and clear water. One of the deepest divers, diving to depths of nearly 200 feet (61 m) to find and feed on its primary foods—mollusks and crustaceans.

A monogamous breeder and solitary nester. Does not breed until it reaches 2-3 years of age. Male leaves the female when she starts to incubate and joins with other males in large flocks to molt, acquiring non-breeding (eclipse) plumage.

Ducklings leave the nest shortly after hatching and follow their mother to water. The young find their own food, but are attended by their mother. Young gather in groups (crèches) during the day and are watched by other females while the mothers feed. Able to take flight at 50-55 days of age.

Ross's Goose
Chen rossii

MIGRATION

Size: L 21-25" (53-63 cm); WS 4' (1.2 m);
WT 2 lb. 12 oz. (1.2 kg)

Male: Occurs in two color morphs. White morph is all
white, except for black wing tips. Pink-to-red bill,
legs and feet. Dark morph is nearly black overall,
with a white belly and face. Pink or light red bill,
legs and feet. Both morphs have a stubby bill.

Female: same as male

Juvenile: white morph is overall white with black wing
tips; dark morph ranges from overall dull gray to
black with a white belly; both have a dark bill,
legs and feet

Food: roots and shoots of aquatic plants, aquatic insects,
berries, grains

Habitat: wet meadows, lakes, corn fields, pastures, prairies

Sounds: both sexes give a low grunting call with squeal-
ing notes; less vocal than the Snow Goose

Compare: White morph Ross's is much smaller than the Tundra
Swan (pg. 179) and Trumpeter Swan (pg. 187), both of which
lack the black wing tips. American White Pelican (pg. 251) is
also white with black wing tips, but it has an enormous bill and
is much larger than Ross's Goose.

Dark morph Ross's has a much shorter neck than Canada Goose
(pg. 171), which has a black neck and white chin strap.

Both morphs of Ross's are very similar to the two Snow Goose
(pg. 167) morphs, but Snow Goose is larger in size and has a
larger orange-to-pink bill.

Flight: strong direct flight with strong, fast wing beats; white morph has a white body and head, short white neck and black wing tips; dark morph has a white belly, head and tail, dark chest, short dark neck and white wings with dark wing tips and thin, dark trailing edges; juvenile is very similar to adult of the same morph

flight pattern

Flock: 1-2 individuals, in large mixed flocks with Snow Geese; V shape or straight-line formation

Migration: complete migrator, to coastal Texas, New Mexico and Mexico

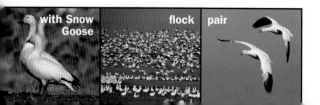

with Snow Goose   flock   pair

Nesting: ground, near the edge of water, on a tussock; female builds with mud and vegetation gathered from the immediate area and lines the nest with grasses and down feathers plucked from her chest and belly; 1 brood

Eggs/Incubation: 3-5 white eggs; female incubates 21-24 days

Fledging: 40-45 days; female and male tend young; goslings copy feeding behavior of parents

Stan's Notes: North America's smallest goose, not commonly found in Minnesota. Usually only one or two individuals seen at a time, mixed in flocks of Snow Geese (pg. 167) during migration. Often migrates in a corridor west of the route used by Snow Geese and spends the winter mostly in Texas and Mexico.

Both Ross's and Snow Goose have two color morphs, but unlike the dark Snow Goose, the dark Ross's is very uncommon. At a distance, white and dark Ross's can be distinguished from Snow Goose morphs by the smaller size and shorter neck. In flight, the Ross's has a faster wing beat than the Snow Goose.

A monogamous breeder. Females don't breed until the third year, and one- and two-year-old individuals don't participate in nesting when families arrive back on nesting grounds together. Although the female does all the incubating, the male attends her during incubation and helps guard the young after they hatch. Goslings leave the nest shortly after hatching and do not return to the nest.

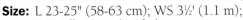

Cackling Goose
Branta hutchinsii

MIGRATION
WINTER

Size: L 23-25" (58-63 cm); WS 3½' (1.1 m); WT 3 lb. 8 oz. (1.6 kg)

Male: Gray goose with a small, rounded black head and white chin or cheek strap. Short black neck. Very short black bill. White rump and undertail. Black legs, feet and tail.

Female: same as male

Juvenile: same as adult

Food: aquatic plants, insects, seeds, sedges, berries, bulbs, grains

Habitat: marshes, lakes, prairies, agricultural fields

Sounds: both sexes honk loudly and give a high-pitched squeaking call in flight or during a confrontation; honking is very similar to that of Canada Goose, but slightly higher pitched; can be heard anytime of year

Compare: The Cackling Goose is smaller and less common than the Canada Goose (pg. 171), with a shorter neck and smaller, stubbier bill. Also smaller than the Greater White-fronted Goose (pg. 163), which lacks the black neck and white chin strap.

The Cackling Goose can be seen mostly during migration. Check for the short neck, small rounded head and very short bill to help identify this small-bodied goose.

Flight: strong direct flight with deep wing beats; both sexes have a brown belly, black-tipped tail, obvious white patch under the tail, short neck and small head

flight pattern

Flock: 2-200 individuals, usually in mixed flocks with Canada Geese; small V-shaped formation, one side sometimes longer than the other, or in a long single string, with each individual slightly off to the side of the one it follows

Migration: non-migrator to partial, to southern states and Texas; some move only far enough south in winter to find open water

with Canad Goos

Nesting: platform, near the edge of water, on the ground; female builds a large mound with plant material gathered from the immediate area and lines the nest with down feathers plucked from her chest and belly; 1 brood

Eggs/Incubation: 5-10 white eggs; female incubates 25-30 days

Fledging: 42-55 days; male and female tend young; goslings feed instinctively

Stan's Notes: The Cackling Goose was recently separated into its own species. Formerly considered a subspecies of the Canada Goose (*B. canadensis*) (pg. 171), it is now *B. hutchinsii*, one of four subspecies in a small-bodied group. Seven other subspecies of Canada Goose are now in a large-bodied group. Despite the two neat groupings, it is often hard to tell the difference between the groups and extremely difficult to differentiate among subspecies.

There are significant differences, however, in the voices of the two groups. Calls of small-bodied geese are generally higher in pitch than those of the larger bodied birds. Calls of large-bodied geese are deeper.

The neck of Cackling Goose is shorter than that of Canada Goose, but when an individual holds its neck down in a relaxed position or extends it while alert and looking around, the length may be hard to judge. The small size of the bill is a good indicator of this species when a goose is nearby, less from a distance.

Most Cackling Geese are seen in Minnesota in spring and autumn, when they move through the state during migration. Some may remain here for the winter.

Brant
Branta bernicla

RARE

Size: L 25" (63 cm); WS 3½' (1.1 m); WT 3 lb. 1 oz. (1.4 kg)

Male: A large black, white and gray goose. Black head and neck with a white necklace just beneath the chin. Small dark bill. Belly ranges from light gray to black. White rump and tail, with a black edge on tail. Black legs and feet.

Female: same as male

Juvenile: similar to adult by the first summer

Food: aquatic grasses and insects, sedges, mosses, seeds, lichens, mollusks

Habitat: prairie wetlands, large lakes, agricultural fields

Sounds: both sexes give a throaty "cronk" call; flock in flight makes a constant, low murmuring sound

Compare: Brant is smaller than the Greater White-fronted Goose (pg. 163), which lacks the black head and neck and white necklace. Canada Goose (pg. 171) has a white cheek patch instead of a white necklace and is overall less dark than the Brant.

Look for the Brant in Minnesota during fall migration and winter. Almost always in small to large flocks, except when an individual gets separated from the flock and is lost. To help identify, look for the black head and neck with a white necklace.

juvenile

adult

Flight: rapid direct flight with strong wing beats; both sexes have a gray belly and wings, dark neck and head, bold white rump and black-tipped tail

flight pattern

Flock: 2-200 individuals; large mass in straight-line, irregular V or other formation, flying high up over land and water with other goose species, often changing leaders, giving the appearance of no particular leader

Migration: complete migrator, to the Atlantic and Pacific coasts, the Great Lakes and Mexico

light belly   black belly   adult   pair

Nesting: ground, near the water, often on islands, in a shallow depression; female builds with mosses, lichens and bits of seaweed gathered from the immediate area and lines the nest with down feathers plucked from her chest and belly; 1 brood

Eggs/Incubation: 4-8 pale white eggs; female incubates 22-26 days

Fledging: 40-50 days; female and male lead young to food; goslings copy feeding behavior of parents

Stan's Notes: Only occasionally seen during fall and winter in Minnesota. A coastal bird that spends most of its time on shallow bays and marshes when wintering and breeding. Almost always seen in flocks feeding in the water or flying in large, irregular V-shaped formations with other goose species.

A monogamous breeder that may mate for life. Female usually nests in a slight depression lined with mosses, lichens, seaweed, and down feathers from her chest and belly. When not incubating, she covers her eggs temporarily with more downy feathers before she leaves the nest. Relatively tame, the female holds tight to her nest when approached, laying low and extending her neck out in front to blend with her surroundings.

Three varieties (morphs) in North America—light, intermediate and black—all with very similar plumage. Morphs intermingle freely on breeding grounds, but migrate to different wintering grounds. Light morphs winter along the Atlantic coast and the Great Lakes. Intermediates spend the winter at Puget Sound in Washington. Black morphs winter on the Pacific coast of California and Mexico.

Brants form loose colonies to migrate and nest. Nearly half of the nesting population can be found on the tundra of the Yukon-Kuskokwim Delta; the rest nest farther north along coastal Alaska.

Greater White-fronted Goose

Anser albifrons

MIGRATION

Size: L 28" (71 cm); WS 4½' (1.4 m); WT 4 lb. 14 oz. (2.2 kg)

Male: Grayish brown bird with a distinctive white band at base of bill. Light pink-to-orange bill. Irregular black barring on the chest and belly. White rump and undertail. Orange legs and feet.

Female: same as male

Juvenile: lighter color than adult, with a yellowish bill, legs and feet

Food: aquatic plants and insects, grains, mosses, sedges, lichens

Habitat: prairies, agricultural fields, marshes, ponds, lakes

Sounds: both sexes give a high-pitched honk or yelp; flock in flight gives continuous calls that are higher and clearer than those of Canada Geese

Compare: The Greater White-fronted has a similar size as Snow Goose (pg. 167). Dark morph Snow Goose has a dark gray body and usually a white head. White morph Snow Goose is entirely white, except for black wing tips, and has an orange-to-pink bill. Swan Goose (pg. 177) is larger and has a two-toned neck and large knob on its forehead. Brant (pg. 159) has a black head and neck with a white necklace. Graylag Goose (pg. 175) is larger, lacks barring on its chest and belly and is common in barnyards. The Canada Goose (pg. 171) is also larger and has a black neck and cheek strap.

Greater White-fronted Geese usually will be in mixed flocks with Snow Geese and Canada Geese. Look for the white band at the base of bill, dark barring on the chest and belly and orange legs to help identify the White-fronted.

Flight: steady direct flight with rapid, shallow wing beats; both sexes have long, narrow gray wings, a contrasting brown body, chest and neck, an obvious U-shaped white rump and undertail with a black band near the tip of tail, and yellow legs and feet; juvenile is similar to adult, lacks the black barring on belly; legs and feet tuck against the body during longer flights

flight pattern

Flock: 2-200 individuals, often in flocks with Snow and Canada Geese; large V or straight-line formation, flying high in the sky

Migration: complete migrator, to coastal Texas, New Mexico, California and Mexico

Nesting: ground, near the water, in a depression; female lines the depression with seaweed gathered from the immediate area and down feathers plucked from her chest and belly; 1 brood

Eggs/Incubation: 4-7 creamy white eggs; female incubates 23-25 days

Fledging: 40-45 days; male and female tend young; goslings feed instinctively

Stan's Notes: Hunters often call this goose Speckled-bellied due to the irregular marking on its belly. Frequently stands in fields, feeding on spilled grains. In the water it feeds like a dabbling duck, leaning forward and pulling up shoots of aquatic plants.

Hybridizes with both Snow Geese (pg. 167) and Canada Geese (pg. 171), producing individuals with the characteristics of the parent species. Three varieties in North America, with differences that are subtle and hard to distinguish.

Usually seen only during spring and autumn, more so in autumn when over 1 million birds–more than half of the North American population–migrate through western Minnesota and the Dakotas. Often seen in mixed flocks with Snow Geese and Canada Geese or flying high up in large wedge shapes. Learns migratory route from parents and older members of the flock. More common in some years, less in others.

Does not breed until it reaches 3 years of age. Nests in Alaska and the Canadian Northwest Territories. Young leave the nest shortly after hatching and take their first flight at 40-48 days of age.

Snow Goose
Chen caerulescens

MIGRATION

Size: L 25-38" (63-96 cm); WS 4½' (1.4 m); WT 5 lb. 4 oz. - 7 lb. 8 oz. (2.4-3.4 kg)

Male: Occurs in two color morphs. White morph is all white, except for black wing tips. Dark morph is overall light to dark gray, sometimes with an all-white head. Both morphs have an orange-to-pink bill, legs and feet.

Female: same as male

Juvenile: white morph is overall light gray; dark morph is dark gray; both have a dark bill, legs and feet

Food: roots and shoots of aquatic plants, aquatic insects, berries, grains

Habitat: wet meadows, lakes, corn fields, pastures, prairies

Sounds: both sexes give harsh honks or nasal barks; calls are more raucous than those of other geese; usually calls continuously during flight

Compare: White morph Snow Goose is much smaller than the Tundra Swan (pg. 179) and Trumpeter Swan (pg. 187), both of which lack black wing tips. American White Pelican (pg. 251) is also white with black wing tips, but it has an enormous bill and is much larger than Snow Goose.

Dark morph Snow Goose lacks the black neck and white cheek strap of Canada Goose (pg. 171).

Both of the Snow Goose color morphs are very similar to the two morphs of the Ross's (pg. 151), but Snow Goose is larger, with a larger bill that is orange to pink.

GEESE

167

adult

Flight: strong direct flight with strong wing beats, some gliding; white morph has a white body, head and neck and black wing tips; dark morph has a dark body and neck, and white tail and wings with dark wing tips and dark trailing edges; white and dark morph juveniles are overall gray

flight pattern

Flock: huge flock of 200-20,000 individuals; bunched, in a large V shape or straight-line formation, flying very high in the sky

Migration: complete migrator, to Gulf coast states and Mexico

dark morph · juvenile · flock · small group

Nesting: ground, near the edge of water, on a tussock; female builds with mud and vegetation gathered from the immediate area and lines the nest with grasses and down feathers plucked from her chest and belly; 1 brood

Eggs/Incubation: 3-5 white eggs; female incubates 23-25 days

Fledging: 45-49 days; female and male tend young; goslings copy feeding behavior of parents

Stan's Notes: Two color morphs of this goose–at one time each was considered a separate species. The white morph, with its all-white plumage and black wing tips, is the more common of the two. The dark morph is also known as the blue morph, although its chest and back are gray, not blue. Some dark individuals have an all-white head. Both morphs have orange-to-pink legs and feet, and a color-coordinated thick serrated bill that helps the bird pull up aquatic vegetation.

A monogamous breeder, maybe for life, with females starting to breed at 2-3 years of age. Older females produce more eggs and are more successful at brooding than younger females. Goslings leave the nest soon after hatching and are attended by the parents. Young take their first flight at 40-48 days of age.

Usually seen only during migration, less during spring and much more in fall, when hundreds to thousands of birds move through the state. In autumn they are heading down to Gulf coast states to spend the winter. During spring they are returning to breeding grounds on tundra in northern Canada. Snow Geese return to the exact same spot for breeding each year, but often take a different migratory route, depending on weather and wind.

Both Snow Goose color morphs travel together in mixed flocks, but tend to segregate when they get to their breeding grounds. Often seen with Ross's Geese (pg. 151) and Sandhill Cranes (not shown) during migration.

Canada Goose

Branta canadensis

YEAR-ROUND
SUMMER

Size: L 25-43" (63-109 cm); WS 5½' (1.7 m); WT 4-10 lb. (1.8-4.5 kg)

Male: Large gray goose with a black neck and head and white chin or cheek strap. White rump and under-tail. Black bill, legs and feet.

Female: same as male

Juvenile: same as adult

Food: aquatic plants, insects, seeds

Habitat: wide variety of ponds, lakes and rivers, often in suburban locations or large wildlife management areas

Sounds: both sexes give a loud honking call, often while in flight or during a confrontation; will hiss when threatened; can be heard anytime of year

Compare: Canada Goose is larger than the Greater White-fronted Goose (pg. 163), which lacks the black neck and white chin strap. Smaller than the Swan Goose (pg. 177), which has a two-toned neck and large knob on its forehead. The dark morph Snow Goose (pg. 167) has a small orange-pink bill, often has an all-white head and is smaller than the Canada Goose. Cackling Goose (pg. 155) is also smaller, with a smaller, rounder head, shorter neck and very short bill. Brant (pg. 159) has a white necklace instead of the white cheek strap of the Canada Goose.

Flight: strong direct flight with deep wing beats; both sexes have a brown belly, dark neck and head, white cheek strap, black tip of tail and an obvious white patch under the tail; neck is outstretched

flight pattern

Flock: 3-3,000 individuals; small to large V-shaped formation, one side sometimes longer than the other, or in a long single string, with each individual slightly off to the side of the one it follows

Migration: non-migrator to partial, to southern states

variant
flock

Nesting: platform, near the water, on the ground; female builds a large mound with plant material gathered from the immediate area and lines the nest with down feathers plucked from her chest and belly; 1 brood

Eggs/Incubation: 5-10 white eggs; female incubates 25-30 days

Fledging: 42-55 days; male and female tend young; goslings feed instinctively

Stan's Notes: Also called Honker. A year-round resident in parts of Minnesota, moving around the state to find open water and a constant supply of food. Many move during autumn to Rochester, where hundreds of thousands of Canada Geese spend the winter.

The Canada Goose was eliminated from Minnesota in the 1930s and early 1940s. It was reintroduced to federal refuges in the late 1940-50s, and to local and state lands in the 1960-70s. Once not too common, it has adapted to our changed environment well.

Adults mate every year, but do not start breeding until their third year. Parents with goslings will take young from other parents by force or adopt orphaned goslings, sometimes resulting in one set of parents caring for as many as 24 goslings. Adults molt primary flight feathers while raising their young, rendering family groups flightless simultaneously.

Males often act as sentinels, standing at the edge of the group and bobbing their heads up and down, becoming very aggressive to anyone approaching. Will hiss as though displaying displeasure.

Characteristics of several subspecies vary across the U.S. Eastern groups generally have a paler color than western groups, which are darker. Size decreases going northward, with the smallest subspecies seen on the Arctic tundra. Until recently, the Cackling Goose (pg. 155) was a subspecies of the Canada Goose, but new DNA evidence shows it to be a separate species. Occasionally variants occur with a white forehead or dark cheeks.

white

Graylag Goose
Anser anser

DOMESTIC

Size: L 34" (86 cm); WS 4-4½' (1.2-1.4 m);
WT 5-7 lb. (2.3-3.2 kg)

Male: Overall light brown goose with a white belly, rump and undertail. Wedge-shaped orange-to-pink bill, trimmed in white at the base. Orange yellow legs and feet. May be partly to mostly white.

Female: same as male

Juvenile: similar to adult

Food: aquatic plants, grains, seeds, grasses

Habitat: barnyards, city parks, golf courses, petting zoos, ponds, lakes, rivers

Sounds: both sexes give loud rancorous honks or cackles

Compare: The Graylag is larger and bulkier than Greater White-fronted Goose (pg. 163), which has dark barring on its chest and belly. Also larger than the Brant (pg. 159), which is black, white and gray with a white necklace. The Canada Goose (pg. 171) has a black neck and white chin strap.

Stan's Notes: Not native to Minnesota, originally from Europe and Asia. The ancestral species of most domesticated geese seen today. Usually unafraid of people and will approach, looking for food. Normally found in groups of 2-5 individuals, often mixing in with other domesticated ducks and geese that were released on area ponds and lakes. Mostly seen with large-bodied Domestic Mallards (pg. 87).

Generally not found in flocks of wild geese, and not much of a sustainable wild breeding population in the state. A Graylag seen in the wild most likely has escaped from captivity, such as from a breeder or barnyard, or was released. *Domestic species—2 pages only*

black knob

Swan Goose
Anser cygnoides

DOMESTIC

Size: L 45" (114 cm); WS 3½-4' (1.1-1.2 m);
WT 9-11 lb. (4.1-5 kg)

Male: Overall light brown to tan with a long neck, light tan on the front and dark brown on the back. Black bill with a large black knob on forehead, sometimes trimmed in orange. Large white rump and tail. Orange legs and feet.

Female: same as male, but slightly smaller with a smaller knob on forehead

Juvenile: similar to adult

Food: aquatic plants, grains, seeds, grasses

Habitat: barnyards, city parks, golf courses, petting zoos, ponds, lakes, rivers

Sounds: both sexes give loud rancorous honks similar to other geese

Compare: Graylag Goose (pg. 175) is smaller than Swan Goose and has an orange bill trimmed in white.

Stan's Notes: One of the largest of all geese. Called Swan Goose due to its long neck and graceful swimming. Originally found in Mongolia and eastern Russia, wintering in China. Also known as Chinese Goose. Domesticated many centuries ago and introduced around the world. Can lay up to 75 eggs in one season, making it desirable on farms. A Swan Goose seen in the wild most likely has escaped from captivity, such as from a breeder or barnyard, or was irresponsibly released. Has been known to charge people for no reason, hissing and beating its wings. *Domestic species—2 pages only*

MIGRATION

Tundra Swan
Cygnus columbianus

Size: L 50-54" (127-137 cm); WS 5½' (1.7 m); WT 14-15 lb. (6.3-6.8 kg)

Male: Large, entirely white bird with a long neck. Large black bill. Yellow mark in front of eyes on lore (base of bill), highly variable in size and shape. Mark can be obvious or well hidden. Black legs and feet.

Female: same as male

Juvenile: same size as adult, but plumage is gray and bill is pinkish gray

Food: aquatic plants and insects

Habitat: large lakes, backwaters of large rivers

Sounds: both sexes give a raspy horn-like call and occasional hooting and barking calls; juvenile gives a high-pitched whistling call

Compare: The Tundra Swan is smaller than the Trumpeter Swan (pg. 187), which lacks any yellow on its face. The white morph Snow Goose (pg. 167) is much smaller than the Tundra Swan and has black wing tips. The Mute Swan (pg. 185) is larger, with an orange bill. The American White Pelican (pg. 251) shares the white plumage, but has black wing tips and a huge orange bill.

The Tundra Swan is usually seen only during autumn migration. Look for the black bill with a yellow mark near the eyes to help identify this swan.

Flight: strong direct flight with steady wing beats; both sexes are all white with a long neck; juvenile is the same as adult, but overall gray; neck is outstretched, feet tuck tightly against the body or are hidden by body feathers at the base of tail

flight pattern

Flock: 20-200 individuals; large V or straight-line formation that can be extremely long

Migration: complete migrator, to the Atlantic coast, with many wintering in Chesapeake Bay

adult | yellow mark | group display | adult and juvenile

Nesting: ground, near the edge of water, on a hummock; female and male build with grasses and mosses; 1 brood

Eggs/Incubation: 4-5 creamy white eggs; female and male incubate 35-40 days

Fledging: 60-70 days; female and male lead young to food; chicks copy feeding behavior of parents

Stan's Notes: The smallest and most numerous of our swans. Formerly called Whistling Swan for its call. Given the common name "Tundra" because it nests on open tundra, preferring islets, peninsulas and elevated areas with many ponds and small lakes nearby. Nests in Alaska and northern Canada, not in Minnesota.

Usually seen here only during autumn migration. Migrates south diagonally across North America in fall, flying nonstop for 2-3 days from Alaska to North Dakota and Minnesota. Gathers in great numbers up to thousands in large lakes and rivers to rest and feed, often staying until the water freezes before continuing to migrate. Flies another 2-3 days to wintering areas on the East coast. Often returns by a different route, flying north up the eastern seaboard, then turning west across northern Canada.

Has a relatively short neck compared with other swans, appearing more goose-like. Tips forward in water to feed, using its long neck to tear off aquatic plants from the bottom. To achieve takeoff, it needs to run along the water's surface for a distance.

Male displays to the female with a high-stepping walk, arching and lifting his neck and stretching out his wings. Mates bow to each other and call constantly during courtship. Minutes later, the pair may fly to a nearby area to court again. Pairs form in the fall before migration, with bonds lasting many years, if not for life.

Female does the most incubation. Chicks are lead to water within hours of hatching and stay with parents for a year. Young are distinguished from adults by their gray plumage and pinkish bills.

with
Canada Geese

Whooper Swan
Cygnus cygnus

DOMESTIC

Size: L 59" (150 cm); WS 7-8' (2.1-2.4 m);
WT 20-22 lb. (9-9.9 kg)

Male: Large, entirely white bird with a long neck. Large black bill with a large lemon yellow patch at the base and on lore (base of bill). Black legs and feet.

Female: same as male

Juvenile: same size as adult, but plumage is gray and base of bill is pale pinkish

Food: aquatic plants and insects

Habitat: barnyards, farms, city ponds, occasionally lakes

Sounds: the loudest and noisiest of swans; both sexes give a loud bugle-like call; wings produce a whistling sound during flight

Compare: Whooper Swan is slightly smaller than the Trumpeter Swan (pg. 187), which lacks the yellow patch on its bill. White morph Snow Goose (pg. 167) has black wing tips and is much smaller. Tundra Swan (pg. 179) is smaller, more common and has an entirely black bill with a yellow mark in front of its eyes on the lore. Mute Swan (pg. 185) is similar in size and shape, but has an orange bill with a black knob at the base.

Stan's Notes: Uncommon in Minnesota. Imported by private collectors, the Whooper is the Eurasian version of our native Trumpeter Swan (pg. 187). All Whoopers in the wild presumably have escaped from captivity or were released.

Holds its neck rigidly while swimming, displaying its large black bill with the flashy yellow base. Like other swans, it needs to run across the water for a distance to take flight. Has a long-term pair bond, with pairs staying together for life or until one mate dies or is killed. Males are called cobs, females are known as pens and young under 1 year of age are cygnets. *Domestic species—2 pages only*

Mute Swan
Cygnus olor

DOMESTIC

Size: L 60" (152 cm); WS 6¼' (1.9 m); WT 22 lb. (9.9 kg)

Male: Large, entirely white bird with a long neck. Large orange bill with a prominent black knob at the base. Black lore (base of bill). Black legs and feet. Holds neck in an S, pointing bill toward the water's surface. Often swims with wings arched.

Female: same as male

Juvenile: same size as adult, but plumage is overall brown to gray and bill is gray with a black base, lacking a prominent knob

Food: aquatic plants and insects

Habitat: ponds, lakes, parks, private property

Sounds: usually silent, but not mute; both sexes will hiss, bark and snort when agitated

Compare: The Mute Swan is nearly the same size as Trumpeter Swan (pg. 187), but Trumpeter has an all-black bill. Tundra Swan (pg. 179) has a black bill with a yellow mark in front of its eyes on the lore and is usually seen only during autumn migration. The white morph Snow Goose (pg. 167) has black wing tips, a much smaller size than Mute and is usually seen in huge flocks.

Stan's Notes: An introduced Eurasian species, frequently seen at lakes, parks, zoos, golf courses and private property. Initially introduced into the Hudson River and Long Island, New York, area by affluent Europeans. Established itself along the Atlantic coast, then moved westward to the Great Lakes. Now found in the wild. Breeding pairs defend large territories, driving off native swans, geese and any other large birds. Some states work to reduce the number of Mute Swans due to the fear of competition with native species. *Domestic species—2 pages only*

Trumpeter Swan
Cygnus buccinator

YEAR-ROUND
MIGRATION
SUMMER

Size: L 60" (152 cm); WS 6½' (2 m); WT 23 lb. (10.4 kg)

Male: Large, entirely white bird with a long neck. Large all-black bill and black lore (base of bill). Black legs and feet.

Female: same as male

Juvenile: same size as adult, but plumage is gray and bill is pinkish gray

Food: aquatic plants and insects

Habitat: backwaters of large rivers, small to large lakes

Sounds: both sexes give a trumpet-like call while defending territory or when threatened; juvenile gives a high-pitched, toy trumpet-like call during flight or while swimming

Compare: Trumpeter Swan is very similar to the Tundra Swan (pg. 179), which is smaller and has a yellow mark in front of its eyes on the lore. White morph Snow Goose (pg. 167) is much smaller than the Trumpeter and has black wing tips. Mute Swan (pg. 185) is nearly the same size, but it has an orange bill with a prominent black knob at the base. The American White Pelican (pg. 251) is similar in size, but has a huge orange bill and black wing tips.

The Trumpeter is a resident swan in Minnesota that can be found in spring, summer and autumn. Usually seen in pairs or with young Trumpeters, which can be identified by their gray plumage and pinkish gray bills.

Flight: strong direct flight with steady wing beats; both sexes are all white with a long neck; juvenile is the same as adult, but overall gray; neck is outstretched, feet tuck tightly against the body or are hidden by body feathers at the base of tail

flight pattern

Flock: 2-10 individuals, in small family groups or pairs; straight-line or V-shaped formation, flying high in the sky

Migration: partial migrator to complete, to southern states; some remain in Minnesota during winter on rivers with open water

adult | black lore | juvenile

Nesting: ground, at the water's edge, often atop a muskrat lodge or mound; female and male build with aquatic vegetation; 1 brood

Eggs/Incubation: 4-6 creamy white eggs; female incubates 33-37 days

Fledging: 100-120 days; female and male tend young; cygnets copy feeding behavior of parents

Stan's Notes: The Trumpeter Swan is the largest member of the waterfowl group in North America and the largest swan in the world. Common name comes from its trumpet-like call.

Was once nearly eliminated from Minnesota due to egg and feather collecting and market hunting. When reintroduction efforts began, its population statewide was estimated to be just a few thousand birds. Reintroduced with great success. Often seen with the large colored neck or wing tags that identify reintroduced individuals.

Unlike Tundra Swans (pg. 179), Trumpeters are usually found in fresh water. Many flock to open water on the Mississippi River in winter, near Monticello. Needs a long expanse of water to take off and land due to its large size. Faces into the wind and runs along the surface of water while flapping to take flight.

When swimming, holds its neck with a slight bend or kink at the base. Tips forward to feed, using its long neck to reach the lake bottom, and tears off vegetation with its powerful bill. The head and upper part of neck are often stained rusty brown from the lake bottom mud.

Forms a pair bond in fall that may last the entire life of the birds. During courtship, mates face each other, raise spread wings, bob their heads and give loud trumpeting calls. Pairs build large nests at the water's edge, often on a mound or muskrat lodge, and defend large territories. Cygnets leave the nest within 1 day of hatching and don't ride the backs of swimming adults. Young stay with their parents until the next breeding season, when they are driven off.

Eared Grebe
Podiceps nigricollis

MIGRATION
SUMMER

Size: L 13" (33 cm); WS 18-20" (45-50 cm); WT 11 oz. (312 g)

Male: Head, neck and back are overall dark brown to black. Sides and chest are chestnut brown. Wispy yellow plumes ("ears") feather out in back of red eyes. Small, slightly upturned black bill. Non-breeding (Oct-Mar) chin and sides are dirty brown to black and white. Dark-tipped gray bill.

Female: same as male

Juvenile: similar to non-breeding adult, with more brown on the chest and neck

Food: fish, aquatic insects, crustaceans, amphibians

Habitat: prairie pothole lakes, small lakes, ponds

Sounds: usually silent; both sexes give shrills, chittering notes and a plaintive, high-pitched call during courtship that repeats many times

Compare: Eared Grebe is slightly smaller than the Horned Grebe (pg. 199), which has a rufous neck and bold yellow tuft behind its eyes instead of wispy yellow plumes. The Red-necked Grebe (pg. 203) is larger, with white cheeks and chin and a black cap. Pied-billed Grebe (pg. 195) is the same size, but has a distinctive black ring around its bill and lacks the yellow "ears." American Coot (pg. 219) is slightly larger, with a short white bill.

Look for a small dark bird with wispy yellow plumes behind its eyes to help identify the Eared Grebe.

non-breeding

Flight: direct flight with rapid, shallow wing beats; both sexes have a white belly, nearly white wing linings, darker wing tips and a long dark neck; neck is outstretched, legs and feet extend beyond the tail

flight pattern

Flock: usually flies alone or in pairs; doesn't fly in flocks during the day

Migration: complete migrator, to the Pacific and Gulf coasts, Mexico and Central America

nesting

Nesting: platform, floating in shallow water, often anchored to vegetation; female and male build with reeds and grasses gathered from the immediate area; 1-2 broods

Eggs/Incubation: 3-5 light blue eggs with brown markings; female and male incubate 20-22 days

Fledging: 20-40 days; male and female feed young

Stan's Notes: A grebe of lakes and ponds in western Minnesota along the Dakota borders. Called Black-necked Grebe in Europe.

Rides higher in water than the Horned Grebe (pg. 199) and Red-necked Grebe (pg. 203). Dives and swims underwater in search of fish and aquatic insects, which make up most of the summer diet. Will often dive underwater to avoid danger, remaining submerged with just its bill exposed above the surface to breathe.

Performs an elaborate courtship display called a penguin dance, with mates in upright positions facing and preening each other. Builds a platform nest in shallow water using reeds and grasses from around the area, frequently anchoring the nest to vegetation. Often builds more than one nest, choosing the one with the best location after all construction is complete.

Chicks leave their nest within 24 hours of hatching. A few days later, they are fed small feathers. Feather eating pads the stomach and is thought to aid the digestion of fish bones and fish. Chicks ride on the backs of swimming parents during their first week. Young siblings are not the same size, since the chicks hatch up to several days apart (asynchronously). Young become independent at 21 days of age.

Nests in large colonies and will gather in large winter flocks, but migrates in small family groups or alone during the night. Many stop in California and Mexico during migration to feed on shrimp-like crustaceans.

Pied-billed Grebe
Podilymbus podiceps

SUMMER

Size: L 13" (33 cm); WS 18-20" (45-50 cm); WT 1 lb. (.5 kg)

Male: Small brown water bird with a black chin and black ring around a thick, chicken-like ivory bill. Puffy white patch beneath the tail. Non-breeding (Sep-Mar) is similar, with a plain brown bill.

Female: same as male

Juvenile: paler than adult, with white spots and gray chest, belly and bill

Food: crayfish, aquatic insects, fish

Habitat: prairie pothole lakes, small to large lakes, ponds

Sounds: male gives loud clucking notes, strung together and lasting 10-15 seconds, to establish territory; male aggression call resembles laughter

Compare: Pied-billed Grebe is the same size as the Eared Grebe (pg. 191), but the Eared has wispy yellow plumes ("ears") on its head and is much less common. The Horned Grebe (pg. 199) is slightly larger and has a yellow tuft behind its eyes. Red-necked Grebe (pg. 203) has a distinctive white cheek patch.

Check for a puffy white patch beneath the tail and thick chicken-like bill to help identify the Pied-billed Grebe.

breeding

non-breeding

Flight: direct flight with rapid, shallow wing beats; both sexes have a small white patch on the belly and light gray wing linings; neck is outstretched, legs and feet extend beyond the tail

Flock: usually flies alone or in pairs; doesn't fly in flocks during the day

flight pattern

Migration: complete migrator, to southern states, Mexico and Central America

non-breeding | juvenile

Nesting: platform, floating in shallow water, often anchored to vegetation; female and male build with reeds and grasses gathered from the immediate area; 1 brood

Eggs/Incubation: 5-7 bluish white eggs; female and male incubate 22-24 days

Fledging: 22-24 days; female and male feed young

Stan's Notes: A very common water bird during summer, often seen diving headfirst for food. Slowly sinks like a submarine when disturbed, becoming denser than water by quickly compressing its feathers to force air out. Once called Hell-diver because of the length of time it is able to remain submerged. Can surface far from where it went under, or just expose the top of its head and bill to take a breath and retreat underwater without being noticed.

Well suited to life on water, with short wings, lobed toes, and legs set close to the rear of its body. Swims easily, but very awkward on land. Also very sensitive to pollution.

Does not use an upright posture when courting, like other grebe species. Strikes an inviting head pose instead, indicating readiness to mate. Sometimes the female mounts the male (reverse mounting), which apparently strengthens the pair bond.

Covers the eggs with vegetation before leaving the nest. Eggs need to lose water content during incubation, which is a problem since most Pied-billed nests are soggy or wet. However, the eggs have up to three times more pores for water diffusion compared with eggs of other species that have similar sizes. Young leave the nest within 24 hours after hatching and will ride on the backs of their swimming parents for up to a week.

Horned Grebe
Podiceps auritus

MIGRATION
SUMMER
WINTER

Size: L 14" (36 cm); WS 18" (45 cm); WT 1 lb. (.5 kg)

Male: Overall reddish with a black head and rufous red neck and sides. Yellow tuft behind red eyes. Dark back. Small black bill with a tiny white mark at the tip. Non-breeding (Sep-Mar) has a black cap, white face, chin and neck and gray bill with a white tip.

Female: same as male

Juvenile: similar to non-breeding adult

Food: fish, aquatic insects

Habitat: prairie pothole lakes, small lakes, ponds

Sounds: both sexes give a series of twitters and chatters, usually reserved for defending territory at the breeding grounds

Compare: The Horned Grebe is slightly larger than Eared Grebe (pg. 191), which has a black neck and wispy yellow plumes ("ears") instead of a bold yellow tuft on each side of its head. The Red-necked Grebe (pg. 203) is larger, with a bright white chin and cheeks and larger bill. Pied-billed Grebe (pg. 195) is slightly smaller and lacks the yellow tuft behind its eyes and rufous neck.

Look for the bold black head with yellow tufts on either side to help identify the Horned Grebe.

Flight: direct flight with rapid, shallow wing beats; both sexes have a distinctive white belly, pale white wing linings, darker wing tips and white wing patch (speculum); neck is outstretched, legs and feet extend beyond the tail

flight pattern

Flock: usually flies alone or in pairs; doesn't fly in flocks during the day

Migration: complete migrator, to the Atlantic, Pacific and Gulf coasts

non-breeding

Nesting: platform, floating in shallow water, often anchored to vegetation; female and male build with reeds and grasses gathered from the immediate area; 1 brood

Eggs/Incubation: 3-5 light blue eggs with light markings; female and male incubate 22-25 days

Fledging: 20-40 days; male and female feed young

Stan's Notes: One of seven grebe species in North America; all species are found in Minnesota except Least Grebe (not shown). The Horned Grebe is a bird of small lakes and ponds in western Minnesota. Spends the summer in fresh water and winters in both fresh water and salt water.

The common name "Horned" refers to the tuft of yellow feathers behind each eye, seen during its breeding season from April to August. Like the other grebes, it eats feathers–enough to create a feather ball that fills nearly half the stomach.

Will often dive underwater to avoid danger, swimming as far as 500 feet (152 m) before resurfacing. Can remain underwater for up to several minutes.

Performs an elaborate courtship display called rushing, similar to that of Western Grebe (pg. 207) and Clark's Grebe (pg. 211). The male and female quickly rise up side by side from the water and run (rush) across the surface. Shaking their heads, they give weeds to each other as presents (weed dance).

Nests solitarily or sometimes in small colonies of 4-8 pairs. Builds a platform nest in shallow water, often anchoring it to vegetation, continuing construction even while the female lays eggs. Chicks hatch several days apart (asynchronously). Young ride the backs of swimming parents during the first week after hatching. Able to fly at 48-60 days of age.

Red-necked Grebe

Podiceps grisegena

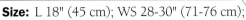

MIGRATION
SUMMER

Size: L 18" (45 cm); WS 28-30" (71-76 cm); WT 2 lb. 2 oz. (1 kg)

Male: Bold black cap, white cheek patch, rusty red neck and brown body. Long, thin bicolored bill, with a yellow lower mandible and dark upper. Non-breeding (Sep-Mar) is overall brown with a slightly darker head, lighter neck and yellow bill.

Female: same as male

Juvenile: similar to non-breeding adult

Food: aquatic insects, small fish, amphibians

Habitat: small ponds, shallow lakes lined with reeds and sedges

Sounds: both sexes give a loon-like call; male call is higher pitched than the female call; courting male gives nasal quacks and low grunting notes

Compare: The Red-necked Grebe is larger than the Eared Grebe (pg. 191), which has a black neck and wispy yellow plumes that feather out behind its eyes. Horned Grebe (pg. 199) is smaller, with a yellow tuft behind its eyes and a smaller bill. Pied-billed Grebe (pg. 195) is also smaller and lacks the black cap and white cheek patch. American Coot (pg. 219) is much more common and lacks the white cheek patch and rusty red neck.

Look for the bold black and white head with a rusty red neck to help identify the Red-necked Grebe.

pair

Flight: direct flight with rapid, shallow wing beats; both sexes have an obvious white belly and chest, red neck, gray wing linings, darker gray wing tips, white on inner leading and trailing edges of wings and obvious white wing patch (speculum); neck is outstretched, legs and feet extend beyond the tail

flight pattern

Flock: usually flies alone or in pairs; doesn't fly in flocks during the day

Migration: complete migrator, to the Atlantic, Pacific and Gulf coasts

Nesting: platform, floating in shallow water, often anchored to vegetation; female and male build with reeds and grasses gathered from the immediate area; 1 brood

Eggs/Incubation: 3-6 white eggs; female and male incubate 21-23 days

Fledging: 50-70 days; female and male feed young

Stan's Notes: The Red-necked is the only grebe species that has white inner leading and trailing edges of wings. Like the other grebes, the Red-necked has a tiny tail, usually hidden in the fluffy feathers at the base (coverts). It has lobed toes unlike the ducks, which have webbed feet.

Forages for food by diving for small fish and aquatic insects, often remaining underwater for up to a minute. Will gather in small feeding groups of as many as 10 birds on large lakes in summer. Often seen near gatherings of loons during late summer.

Doesn't fly much once at nesting grounds. Builds a floating nest with plants and anchors it to one spot; this type of nest does not submerge when water rises during spring snowmelt. Tends to be rather shy, especially around the nest.

Chicks hatch one day at a time (asynchronously). Parents feed tiny feathers to their young 1-2 days after hatching. The feathers presumably help protect the stomach lining from bones in fish, its main diet.

The common name "Grebe" probably came from the Old English krib, meaning "crest," a reference to the crested head plumes of many grebe species, especially during the breeding season. Grebe populations have decreased over the past 30 years, possibly due to pesticides, increased predation of eggs and habitat loss.

OTHER
WATER BIRDS

Western Grebe
Aechmophorus occidentalis

MIGRATION
SUMMER

Size: L 24" (60 cm); WS 26-30" (66-76 cm);
WT 3 lb. 4 oz. - 3 lb. 14 oz. (1.5-1.7 kg)

Male: Long-necked water bird with a black crown, nape and back, with black extending from the crown to the base of bill. White chin, throat, chest and belly. Long, thin greenish yellow bill. Bright red eyes. Non-breeding (Sep-Feb) is light gray around the eyes.

Female: same as male

Juvenile: similar to non-breeding adult

Food: fish, aquatic insects

Habitat: small to large lakes

Sounds: both sexes give a 2-part "cree-reek" call throughout summer and a repetitious rattling, raspy call during courtship

Compare: Western Grebe is nearly identical to the Clark's Grebe (pg. 211), but Clark's has a bright yellow bill and white extending higher on its face, above the eyes. The Common Loon (pg. 243) is larger, with a white necklace, black-and-white checkerboard pattern on its back and long black bill. The Red-necked Grebe (pg. 203) is smaller and has a red neck. Horned Grebe (pg. 199) has a yellow tuft behind its eyes. Eared Grebe (pg. 191) has wispy yellow plumes that feather out behind its eyes.

Look for the bold black and white plumage and long, thin greenish yellow bill to help identify the Western Grebe.

non-breeding

Flight: fast direct flight with rapid wing beats; both sexes have a white belly, black axillaries (armpits) and white neck; neck is outstretched, legs and feet extend beyond the tail

flight pattern

Flock: usually flies alone or in pairs; doesn't fly in flocks during the day

Migration: complete migrator, to the Pacific coast, California and Mexico

rushing | weed dance

Nesting: platform, floating in shallow water, often anchored to vegetation; female and male build with reeds and grasses gathered from the immediate area; 1 brood

Eggs/Incubation: 3-4 bluish white eggs with brown markings; female and male incubate 20-23 days

Fledging: 65-75 days; female and male feed young

Stan's Notes: Well known for its unusual breeding dance called rushing. Side by side, with necks outstretched, mates spring to their webbed feet and run (rush) across the surface of the water, diving underwater at the end of the rush. Pairs often hold long stalks of water plants in their bills when courting, presenting the weeds back and forth to each other (weed dance).

Nests in large colonies of as many as 100 pairs on lakes with tall vegetation. Shortly after choosing a large lake for breeding, it rarely flies until early summer. Has a difficult time walking on the ground due to its legs, which are set far back on the body.

Chicks ride on backs of swimming adults, climbing on minutes after hatching. Adults will dive with young on their backs when threatened. Young fly at 65-70 days of age.

Once considered the same species as the Clark's Grebe (pg. 211). Common on some lakes in western Minnesota and nonexistent on others. Was hunted heavily in the late 1800s and early 1900s for its feathers, used to decorate hats, coats and capes. Now loss of habitat and increased predation of eggs are the main reasons for the decline in its population.

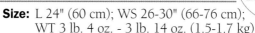

Clark's Grebe
Aechmophorus clarkii

MIGRATION SUMMER

Size: L 24" (60 cm); WS 26-30" (66-76 cm); WT 3 lb. 4 oz. - 3 lb. 14 oz. (1.5-1.7 kg)

Male: Long-necked water bird with a black crown, nape and back, with white extending from the base of bill to above the eyes. White chin, throat, chest and belly. Long, thin bright yellow bill. Bright red eyes. Non-breeding (Sep-Feb) has a small light gray patch above the eyes.

Female: same as male

Juvenile: similar to non-breeding adult

Food: fish, aquatic insects

Habitat: small to large lakes

Sounds: both sexes give a 2-part "cree-reek" call throughout summer and a repetitious rattling, raspy call during courtship

Compare: Clark's Grebe is nearly identical to the Western Grebe (pg. 207), which has a greenish yellow bill and lacks white on its face above the eyes. The Common Loon (pg. 243) is larger, with a white necklace, black-and-white checkerboard pattern on its back and long black bill. Red-necked Grebe (pg. 203) is smaller and has a rusty red neck. Horned Grebe (pg. 199) has a yellow tuft behind its eyes. The Eared Grebe (pg. 191) has wispy yellow plumes that feather out behind its eyes.

Look for the bold black and white plumage and long, thin bright yellow bill to help identify the Clark's Grebe.

non-breeding

Flight: fast direct flight with rapid wing beats; both sexes have a white belly, black axillaries (armpits) and white neck; neck is outstretched, legs and feet extend beyond the tail

flight pattern

Flock: usually flies alone or in pairs; doesn't fly in flocks during the day

Migration: complete migrator, to the Pacific coast, California and Mexico

Nesting: platform, floating in shallow water, often anchored to vegetation; female and male build with reeds and grasses gathered from the immediate area; 1 brood

Eggs/Incubation: 3-4 bluish white eggs with brown markings; female and male incubate 20-23 days

Fledging: 65-75 days; female and male feed young

Stan's Notes: Clark's Grebe is nearly identical to Western Grebe (pg. 207) and was once considered the same species. Clark's is not as common as the Western and generally is found farther west in the U.S. Lives in both freshwater and saltwater habitats, wintering in large numbers along the Pacific coast.

Well known for its unusual breeding dance called rushing. Side by side, with necks outstretched, mates spring to their webbed feet and run (rush) across the surface of the water, diving underwater at the end of the rush. Pairs often hold long stalks of water plants in their bills when courting, presenting the weeds back and forth to each other (weed dance).

Nests in large colonies of as many as 100 pairs on lakes with tall vegetation. Shortly after choosing a large lake for breeding, it rarely flies until early summer. Has a difficult time walking on the ground due to its legs, which are set far back on the body.

Chicks ride on backs of swimming adults, climbing on minutes after hatching. Adults will dive with young on their backs when threatened. Young fly at 65-70 days of age.

Hunted heavily in the late 1800s and early 1900s for its feathers, which were used to decorate hats, coats and capes. Now loss of habitat and increased predation of eggs are the main reasons for its population decline.

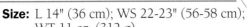

Common Moorhen

Gallinula chloropus

SUMMER

Size: L 14" (36 cm); WS 22-23" (56-58 cm); WT 11 oz. (312 g)

Male: Nearly black overall with a yellow-tipped red bill and red forehead. Thin white line along the sides and a puffy white tail. Long yellowish green legs. Extremely long yellow toes.

Female: same as male

Juvenile: similar to adult, only brown with a brown bill, white throat and dirty yellow legs, lacks the red forehead

Food: aquatic plants, insects, berries, seeds, fruit

Habitat: wetlands, small lakes

Sounds: both sexes give a series of clucks that starts fast and slows near the end with one squeak note between each series, making the call sound like laughter; once one moorhen calls, it seems as though all moorhens in the wetland join the call

Compare: The Moorhen is similar in size to the American Coot (pg. 219), but Coot lacks the distinctive yellow-tipped bill and red forehead and is much more common. Also has a similar size as Horned Grebe (pg. 199), but lacks the yellow tuft behind its eyes. Slightly larger than the Eared Grebe (pg. 191) and lacks the wispy, feathery plumes in back of its eyes.

The Common Moorhen is a very uncommon bird in Minnesota. Look for the yellow-tipped red bill and red forehead to identify.

adult

Flight: swift flight with strong wing beats, weak and fluttering short distance flight; both sexes have an overall gray underside, short rounded wings and yellowish green legs; feet extend well beyond the tail

flight pattern

Flock: usually flies alone or in pairs; doesn't fly in flocks during the day

Migration: complete migrator, to southern coastal states

juvenile   juvenile

Nesting: cup, usually suspended over the water; female and male build with aquatic plants gathered from the immediate area and line the nest with grasses; 1-2 broods

Eggs/Incubation: 2-10 brown eggs with dark markings; female and male incubate 19-22 days

Fledging: 40-50 days; female and male feed young

Stan's Notes: A very uncommon bird in Minnesota, with only a handful of sightings reported in the state. Often seen in southern coastal states, it is much less common as far north as Minnesota.

A secretive bird, often remaining hidden in tall vegetation around shallow lakes and ponds. Also called Pond Chicken and, like the American Coot (pg. 219), Mud Hen (both species nest in muddy ponds, have a chicken-like body shape and bob their heads like chickens when walking). Uses its very long toes to help it walk on floating vegetation, and swims around like a wind-up toy when hunting for insects.

Females are known to lay eggs in the nests of other moorhens in addition to their own. Occasionally takes an old nest that is in a low shrub. Any moorhen nest will be well concealed and some- times has a cover or roof. There are frequently roosting platforms nearby for resting or for brooding the young after they hatch.

A cooperative breeder, with the young of the first brood helping raise the young of the second. Chicks usually leave the nest within a few hours after hatching, but stay with the family for a couple of months. Young ride the backs of swimming adults for a short time until they are too large for the parent. A spur on the wings of young moorhens helps them scramble up vegetation.

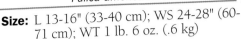

American Coot
Fulica americana

SUMMER

Size: L 13-16" (33-40 cm); WS 24-28" (60-71 cm); WT 1 lb. 6 oz. (.6 kg)

Male: Slate gray to black all over. Short white bill with a dark band near the tip. Long green legs and feet. Small white patch near the base of tail. Prominent red eyes and a small reddish brown patch above the bill between the eyes.

Female: same as male

Juvenile: much paler than adult, with a gray bill

Food: aquatic plants, insects, seeds, tadpoles, snails, crustaceans

Habitat: small to large lakes

Sounds: both sexes give a long string of various grunts, quacks and hoarse notes; male vocalizations tend to be higher in pitch than those made by the female; running over the water's surface produces loud splashing sounds

Compare: American Coot is smaller than most ducks. Common Moorhen (pg. 215) is a similar size, but has a yellow-tipped red bill. The Horned Grebe (pg. 199) also compares in size, but it has yellow tufts on its head. Eared Grebe (pg. 191) is slightly smaller than the Coot and has feathery plumes behind its eyes.

The Coot is the only black water bird or duck-like bird with a white bill. Look for it in large flocks during fall migration.

adult

Flight: fast direct flight with rapid wing beats, weak and fluttering short distance flight; both sexes have a dark underside and short dark wings; feet extend beyond the tail

flight pattern

Flock: up to 2,000 individuals; usually flies alone or in pairs; extremely large flocks float and feed on large lakes from late summer to early fall, but not often seen flying in flocks

Migration: complete migrator, to southern states, Mexico and Central America

diving   juvenile   flock

Nesting: cup, suspended over water or floating in it; female and male build with aquatic vegetation gathered from the immediate area; 1 brood

Eggs/Incubation: 9-12 pinkish buff eggs with brown markings; female and male incubate 21-25 days

Fledging: 49-52 days; female and male feed young

Stan's Notes: Very common in Minnesota and widely distributed over much of North America. Often seen here in extremely large flocks on open water from late summer to early autumn.

Not a duck, as it doesn't have webbed feet. An excellent diver and swimmer, with large lobed toes. Scrambles across the surface of the water when taking off, with wings flapping. Bobs its head like a chicken while swimming. Feeds by tipping forward in shallow water, but dives down to 25 feet (8 m) in deeper water. A fairly noisy bird that communicates with other coots not only with grunts and groans, but also with splashing water.

Male displays for female by paddling after her and flapping his wings. A displaying male may also place his head and neck on the water's surface while raising his wing tips and tail above the surface. An accepting female will strike a similar pose.

Nests are often suspended over water 1-4 feet (.3-1.2 m) deep, in tall vegetation and well concealed. Floating nests are anchored to vegetation. Chicks hatch 1-2 days apart (asynchronously). Young leave the nest within hours of hatching and are cared for by both parents. Young coots start to fly at 50-56 days of age.

The unusual common name "Coot" is of unknown origin, but in Middle English, the word coote was used to describe various water-fowl–perhaps it stuck. Like the Common Moorhen (pg. 215), the American Coot is also called Mud Hen. Both nest in muddy ponds and have the body shape and head movements of a chicken.

male

female

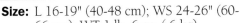

Hooded Merganser
Lophodytes cucullatus

MIGRATION
SUMMER

Size: L 16-19" (40-48 cm); WS 24-26" (60-66 cm); WT 1 lb. 6 oz. (.6 kg)

Male: Sleek black-and-white bird with rust brown sides. Crest "hood" raises, revealing a large white patch. A hammerhead crest, giving the head a unique elongated shape at the back when the crest is down. Long, thin black bill. Yellow eyes. Non-breeding (Jul-Sep) is overall brown and appears very similar to female.

Female: sleek brown and rust bird with a ragged rust crest, long thin brown and yellow bill, yellow eyes

Juvenile: similar to female, with dark eyes

Food: small fish, aquatic insects

Habitat: shallow woodland ponds, sloughs, small lakes, slow-moving rivers

Sounds: male gives a series of pops and clicks; courting male gives a low purring "pah whaaaaaa"; female response is a hoarse croaking call; in flight, wings of male produce a high-pitched insect-like trill

Compare: The male Hooded Merganser is smaller than the male Common Merganser (pg. 231), which has white sides and a green head. Male Bufflehead (pg. 91) is smaller than the Hooded, with white sides. Male Red-breasted Merganser (pg. 227) is larger and has gray sides and a green head. Look for the large white patch on the head and rusty brown sides of the male Hooded.

Female Hooded is smaller than the female Common Merganser (pg. 231), which has a white chin and large orange bill. Female Red-breasted Merganser (pg. 227) is larger and has gray sides and an orange bill. Female Common Goldeneye (pg. 115) is also larger with gray sides, and has a larger, thicker bill and no crest.

female

Flight: rapid direct flight with fast wing beats; male has a light belly and chest and dark head, neck and wings; female has a white belly and dark chest, head, neck and wings; neck is outstretched, feet tuck in during longer flights

flight pattern

Flock: 2-20 individuals; no particular shape or formation

Migration: complete migrator, to southern states and the Gulf coast

male   female   male   juvenile

Nesting: cavity, in an old woodpecker hole or natural cavity in a tree; female lines the cavity with grasses and leaves gathered from the immediate area and down feathers plucked from her chest and belly; 1 brood

Eggs/Incubation: 10-12 white eggs; female incubates 32-33 days

Fledging: 71 days; female tends young; chicks copy feeding behavior of mother

Stan's Notes: Small diving bird of shallow ponds, sloughs, small lakes and slow rivers. Frequently seen in wooded areas, where females nest in natural cavities or nest boxes, but becoming more common in metropolitan areas. Often arrives at nesting grounds in pairs and can be seen in small groups of up to 20 individuals.

The male Hooded raises and lowers his crest at will to show off his large white head patch. During display, he positions himself in front of a female, raises his crest and gives his call. Displaying continues throughout the day and into late evening.

Hoodies hybridize with Common Goldeneyes (pg. 115), producing males with dark heads and smaller crests. Known to share nesting cavities with Common Goldeneyes and also Wood Ducks (pg. 47), sitting side by side.

The female will "dump" her eggs into other female Hooded nests, resulting in 20-25 eggs in some nests. While the female incubates, the male leaves. In late summer, young females scout for nest sites and boxes, presumably in preparation for the coming spring.

male

female

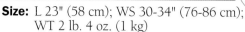

Red-breasted Merganser
Mergus serrator

OTHER WATER BIRDS

YEAR-ROUND
MIGRATION

Size: L 23" (58 cm); WS 30-34" (76-86 cm);
WT 2 lb. 4 oz. (1 kg)

Male: Shaggy green head and crest, rusty red chest and and prominent white collar. Black and white body with gray sides. Long, slender, serrated orange bill with a dark tip (nail) that points downward. Red eyes. Non-breeding (Jun-Oct) looks very similar to the female.

Female: overall gray to light brown with a shaggy reddish orange head and crest, whitish chin and throat, a long, slender, serrated orange bill with a dark nail that points downward, reddish orange eyes

Juvenile: similar to female

Food: fish, aquatic insects, crustaceans

Habitat: large rivers and lakes, both with islands

Sounds: usually silent; female gives a hoarse croak during flight; male sometimes gives a soft cat-like mew

Compare: Male Red-breasted Merganser shares the green head with the male Mallard (pg. 83), but Mallard lacks gray sides and a long pointed bill. Male Common Merganser (pg. 231) has a white chest and sides, is larger than the Red-breasted and more common. Male Hooded Merganser (pg. 223) has a white patch on its crest and is smaller.

Female Red-breasted Merganser is smaller than female Common Merganser (pg. 231), which has a larger orange bill and is more common. The female Hooded Merganser (pg. 223) has a similar shape, but is much smaller, with a brown and yellow bill.

small group

Flight: extremely fast, direct flight with rapid wing beats; male has a white belly, dark chest, neck and head and white wing linings with dark wing tips; female looks very similar to male; body, neck and head are held in a straight line, feet tuck in during longer flights

flight pattern

Flock: 20-200 individuals; straight-line formation or flies alone

Migration: complete migrator, to southern states, the Atlantic, Pacific and Gulf coasts, Mexico and Central America

pair   female   female

Nesting: ground, near the water, usually sheltered beneath the roots of an upturned tree or in a driftwood or log pile, shallow burrow or hollow stump; female builds with plants gathered from the immediate area and lines the nest with down feathers plucked from her chest and belly; 1 brood

Eggs/Incubation: 5-10 olive green eggs; female incubates 29-30 days

Fledging: 55-65 days; female feeds young

Stan's Notes: Breeding resident in northeastern Minnesota and seen throughout the rest of the state during migration. Not nearly as common as the Common Merganser (pg. 231).

The Red-breasted Merganser is an extremely fast flier, clocked at speeds up to 100 mph (161 km/h). Usually seen flying fast and low across the water. Needs a long run with wings flapping for takeoff and getting airborne.

Known to fish in cooperation with other mergansers. Forms a line to drive fish into shallow water, then dives to catch the fish. The serrated bill helps it catch slippery fish.

Female starts to breed after 2 years of age. Male abandons female just after eggs are laid. Females will often share their nests. Chicks leave the nest within 24 hours of hatching, never to return. Young mergansers take their first flight at 60 days of age.

male

female

Common Merganser
Mergus merganser

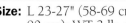

MIGRATION
SUMMER
WINTER

Size: L 23-27" (58-69 cm); WS 32-36" (80-90 cm); WT 3 lb. 6 oz. (1.5 kg)

Male: Long and thin with a large green head and black back. White sides, chest and neck. Long, slender, serrated orange bill with a dark tip (nail) that points downward. Often appears black and white in poor light. Non-breeding (Jul-Oct) looks very similar to the female.

Female: same size and shape as male, but with a rust red head and ragged "hair," gray body, white chest, white chin and long, serrated orange bill with a dark nail that points downward

Juvenile: similar to female, with a small white patch near the base of bill just below eyes

Food: small fish, aquatic insects

Habitat: large to small rivers and lakes

Sounds: female gives a deep repeated quack during flight; courting male gives a deep throaty call

Compare: Male Common Merganser shares the green head with male Mallard (pg. 83), but Mallard lacks the black back, bright white sides and long pointed bill. Male Red-breasted Merganser (pg. 227) has a dark chest, gray sides and is less common. Male Hooded Merganser (pg. 223) is smaller with a large white patch on the head.

Female Common Merganser is larger than female Red-breasted Merganser (pg. 227), which has a smaller, thinner bill, small head and is less common. Female Hooded Merganser (pg. 223) has a similar shape, but is much smaller, with a brown and yellow bill. Look for the reddish head, ragged "hair," orange bill and white chest and chin to help identify the female Common Merganser.

male

Flight: extremely fast, direct flight with rapid, shallow wing beats; male has a white belly, chest and neck, dark head and white wing linings with dark wing tips; female looks very similar to male; body, neck and head are held in a straight line, feet tuck in during longer flights

flight pattern

Flock: 20-2,000 individuals; long straight-line formation, usually flying only 50-100 feet (15-30 m) above the water's surface

Migration: complete migrator, to southern states and Mexico

female   male   non-breeding male

Nesting: cavity, near the water, in an old woodpecker cavity, earthen bank, crevice, wooden box, underneath the roots of an upturned tree or beneath a large rock; female builds a bulky bed with dried plants, roots and mosses gathered from the immediate area and lines nest with down feathers plucked from her chest and belly; 1 brood

Eggs/Incubation: 9-11 ivory eggs; female incubates 28-33 days

Fledging: 70-80 days; female feeds young

Stan's Notes: The Common Merganser is a shallow water diver that feeds mainly on small live fish in 10-15 feet (3-4.5 m) of water. Eats dead fish when the supply of fresh fish is diminished. Catches slippery fish with its serrated bill, which has a fine edge.

More commonly seen along large rivers and lakes than small. In winter, thousands gather on the Mississippi River, wherever open water can still be found.

The female breeds in its second or third year, returning to the same area annually to nest. Some studies show that females have a strong tendency to return to the same nest site.

Similar to the cavity-nesting ducks, female Common Mergansers often lay eggs in other merganser nests (egg dumping), resulting in broods of up to 15 young per mother. When nests contain 20 or more eggs, the eggs on the bottom do not hatch.

Male leaves the female when she starts to incubate. At this time he begins to molt, looking like the female from July through October.

Chicks stay in the nest 24-48 hours after hatching. Orphans are accepted by other merganser mothers with young. During late summer and early fall, large groups of adult females with many young are often seen diving for fish or resting on boat docks and along shorelines.

Red-throated Loon
Gavia stellata

OTHER
WATER BIRDS

MIGRATION

Size: L 25" (63 cm); WS 3-3½' (.9-1.1 m);
WT 3 lb. (1.4 kg)

Male: Overall dark brown to nearly black with a gray
head and neck and obvious red throat. Long, thin
black bill, slightly upturned. Non-breeding (Oct-
Apr) has a white face, neck and chest, gray back
with white spots and lacks the red throat.

Female: same as male

Juvenile: similar to non-breeding adult

Food: fish, aquatic insects, amphibians

Habitat: large lakes such as Lake Mille Lacs and Lake
Superior

Sounds: usually very quiet; both sexes give a short wail or
goose-like quack at the breeding grounds

Compare: The Red-throated is smaller than the Common Loon
(pg. 243), which has a black head, a larger, wider bill and lacks
the red throat. Pacific Loon (pg. 239) is nearly the same size, but
it has a black throat with white stripes on the sides. The Western
Grebe (pg. 207) and Clark's Grebe (pg. 211) are both slightly
smaller, with long white throats and thin yellow bills.

Look for Red-throats on our largest lakes during migration in
spring and fall. Check for them in mixed flocks with Common
Loons, looking for the conspicuous red throat to help identify.

juvenile

Flight: fast direct flight with rapid wing beats; both sexes have a white belly, dark wing linings and head; neck droops slightly below the body, feet extend beyond the tail

flight pattern

Flock: usually flies alone or in pairs; doesn't fly in flocks

Migration: complete migrator, to the Great Lakes, staying until the water freezes, then continues to the Atlantic and Pacific coasts

adult

Nesting: platform, near the edge of water, on the ground; male and female build with grasses and small twigs gathered from the immediate area and line the nest with finer plant material and a few feathers; 1 brood

Eggs/Incubation: 1-3 brown-to-olive eggs; female and male incubate 24-29 days

Fledging: 49-51 days; male and female feed young

Stan's Notes: The smallest of the loons and the only one able to take flight from dry land rather than by running along the water's surface. "Leaps" to flight from both water and land.

The Red-throated is also the only loon species without obvious white marks on its back or neck. Its bill is slightly upturned, unlike the straight bills of other loons, and held upward when swimming.

Often alone except during migration, when hundreds may gather on large lakes. Usually seen at that time in mixed flocks with Common Loons (pg. 243) or other Red-throats. Much less vocal than the Common Loon.

Dives as far as 90 feet (27 m) in search of fish, its primary source of food. Known in Europe as Red-throated Diver.

Splashes around excitedly during courtship, with much display taking place underwater. Nests on smaller lakes and ponds in Alaska and Canada, but not in Minnesota. Unlike other loons, it will nest in small shallow ponds. Usually lays a couple eggs, and remains silent at the nesting grounds. Young hatch up to several days apart and ride on the backs of swimming adults during their first 7-10 days.

When predators or people approach the nest, the adult quietly slips from the nest into the water and resurfaces a safe distance away. Adults also use distraction displays to draw intruders away from their nests and young.

Pacific Loon
Gavia pacifica

MIGRATION

Size: L 25" (63 cm); WS 3-3½' (.9-1.1 m); WT 3 lb. 8 oz. (1.6 kg)

Male: Overall black and white with a large, puffy gray head and gray nape. Black throat with distinctive white vertical stripes on the sides. Black back with a series of white lines or bars. Small, thin black bill. Non-breeding (Sep-Mar) is overall gray to nearly black with white cheeks, chin and throat.

Female: same as male

Juvenile: similar to non-breeding adult, with a grayer head

Food: fish, aquatic insects and plants, amphibians, crustaceans, mollusks

Habitat: large lakes such as Lake Mille Lacs and Lake Superior

Sounds: usually very quiet; male gives a plaintive yodel and long, mournful high-pitched wail at the breeding grounds; both sexes are known to give some guttural quacks and croaks

Compare: Pacific Loon is smaller than Common Loon (pg. 243), which has a black head and larger, wider bill. Red-throated Loon (pg. 235) is nearly the same size, but it has a red throat and lacks black and white stripes on its back. Western Grebe (pg. 207) and Clark's Grebe (pg. 211) are both slightly smaller, with long white throats and thin yellow bills.

Look for the Pacific Loon during migration on any of our large lakes such as Lake Superior.

nesting

Flight: fast direct flight with rapid wing beats; both sexes have a white belly, white and gray wing linings, narrow black axillaries (armpits) and a dark head; neck is outstretched, feet extend beyond tail

flight pattern

Flock: usually flies alone or in pairs; doesn't fly in flocks

Migration: complete migrator, to the Pacific and Gulf coasts; small percentage migrate to the Great Lakes, stay until the water freezes, then continue to the seacoasts

adult and chick

Nesting: platform, at the water's edge, on the ground; male and female build with mud, roots and grasses gathered from the immediate area and line the nest with finer plant material; 1 brood

Eggs/Incubation: 1-3 brown-to-olive eggs; female and male incubate 24-29 days

Fledging: 49-51 days; male and female feed young

Stan's Notes: Pacific Loons are seen on Lake Superior and other large lakes in Minnesota. Once thought to be a subspecies of the very similar-looking Arctic Loon (G. arctica) (not shown), but now considered a separate species. A common bird on the tundra in Alaska and Canada, where it breeds on large shallow lakes.

Head appears large and puffy, and it has a shorter neck than the other loon species. Holds its relatively small bill parallel with the surface of the water when swimming. Can see well both above water and below the surface.

Eats a variety of items such as aquatic insects, crustaceans, frogs, mollusks and aquatic vegetation in summer, but consumes just fish in winter. Unlike other loon species, Pacific adults sometimes fly many miles to hunt for fish in other lakes.

Dips its bill into water repeatedly in a courtship display similar to other loons. Also splashes around a lot before diving, followed by some underwater displays.

Establishes a long-term pair bond, possibly for life, when reproduction is successful. When not successful, a pair may separate to find new mates and nesting grounds. Nests alone or in small groups. Young hatch up to a couple days apart (asynchronously) and leave the nest within hours of hatching.

MIGRATION
SUMMER

Common Loon
Gavia immer

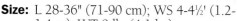

Size: L 28-36" (71-90 cm); WS 4-4½' (1.2-1.4 m); WT 9 lb. (4.1 kg)

Male: Black head with a black-and-white checkerboard patterned back and white necklace. Long, pointed black bill. Deep red eyes. Non-breeding (Sep-Mar) is gray with a white chin and chest and gray bill.

Female: same as male

Juvenile: similar to non-breeding adult, lacks the red eyes

Food: fish, aquatic insects, crayfish

Habitat: large lakes such as Lake Mille Lacs and Lake Superior

Sounds: male gives a yodel, the most common call of the loon; in flight, both sexes often give a series of 5-10 repeating notes known as a tremolo; male and female also wail an all-purpose call, which has a haunting sound similar to the howling of a wolf, and hoot softly to maintain contact with family members nearby

Compare: The most common loon in Minnesota. Larger than the Red-throated Loon (pg. 235), which has a red throat and lacks the black-and-white checkerboard back of Common Loon. Also larger than the Pacific Loon (pg. 239), which has a gray head and white stripes on its back. The Double-crested Cormorant (pg. 247) looks similar, but has a black chest and gray bill with yellow at the base and a hooked tip.

The Common Loon is more likely to be seen than the other loon species in the state. Look for the contrasting black-and-white checkerboard pattern on the back and white-striped necklace.

taking flight

Flight: fast direct flight with rapid wing beats; both sexes have a white belly, nearly white wing linings and a dark head; lower neck droops slightly below the body, wings are held above the plane of the body, feet extend beyond and slightly below the tail

flight pattern

Flock: usually flies alone or in pairs; doesn't fly in flocks

Migration: complete migrator, to the Gulf and Atlantic coasts and Mexico

nesting   juvenile   adult

Nesting: platform, near the edge of water, on the ground; female and male build with aquatic vegetation and grasses gathered from the immediate area; 1 brood

Eggs/Incubation: 2 olive brown eggs, occasionally with brown markings; female and male incubate 26-31 days

Fledging: 75-80 days; female and male feed young

Stan's Notes: The state bird of Minnesota and a testament to our abundant lakes and fish. Its unique call suggests the wild laughter of a demented person and led to the phrase "crazy as a loon." Once thought to require undisturbed lakes, but loons are now living and reproducing successfully on lakes well populated by people.

The common name comes from the Swedish word lom, meaning "lame," for the awkward way it walks on land. Legs are set so far back on the body that it has a hard time walking on land, but it is a great swimmer. Prefers clear lakes because it hunts for fish by eyesight. Spends the winter on salt water, something most freshwater birds don't do due to their inability to digest increased salt. Excretes excess salt through glands located at the base of the bill.

Performs a splashing, diving "penguin dance" during courtship, rising to a vertical position with wings outstretched. Prefers small islands for nesting, but will use an artificial floating platform nest. Young hatch 1-2 days apart (asynchronously), with many parents successfully raising both chicks. Young loons ride on the backs of their swimming parents during the first 7-10 days of life.

Captures tiny fish to feed to chicks. Surfaces partially with only its head above water when feeding young, to be at the same level as the chicks. Passes the catch to the young, who swallow the fish headfirst and whole in the same way that adults eat their food.

Adults perform distraction displays to protect the young. Pairs will drive off other birds on the lake, such as ducks and grebes, until midsummer, when they become less territorial and aggressive.

Double-crested Cormorant

Phalacrocorax auritus

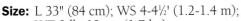

SUMMER

Size: L 33" (84 cm); WS 4-4½' (1.2-1.4 m); WT 3 lb. 12 oz. (1.7 kg)

Male: Large black bird with a long, thin snake-like neck. Plumage has an iridescent green sheen in direct sunlight, apparent when the individual is nearby. Long gray bill with a hooked tip and yellow at the base. Cobalt blue eyes. Black legs and feet. Black (sometimes white) feather plumes on the face just behind the eyes, resembling eyebrows, frequently hidden and difficult to see. Non-breeding (Jun-Dec) lacks the feather plumes behind eyes.

Female: same as male

Juvenile: light brown with a grayish chest and neck, bill is yellowish orange

Food: small fish, aquatic insects, amphibians

Habitat: small to large lakes

Sounds: both sexes give a series of deep guttural grunts and groans that resemble the sounds of a marine mammal such as a seal or walrus

Compare: The Double-crested is twice the size of American Coot (pg. 219), which has a short white bill and lacks the long neck. Common Loon (pg. 243) has a similar size as Double-crested, but it has a black-and-white checkered pattern on its back and long black bill. The Red-throated Loon (pg. 235) is much smaller and less common, with a red throat.

Look for the Double-crested Cormorant at lakes in Minnesota that have plentiful fish. From a distance, look for a black bird with a long neck and other black birds sitting erect with wings outstretched, drying their feathers in the sun. When near and in sunlight, check for the green iridescence of the plumage.

Flight: strong direct flight with rapid, shallow wing beats and some gliding; both sexes have an all-black underside; juvenile is brown with a gray chest and neck; head is held stretched out straight, neck has a distinctive crook

flight pattern

Flock: 2-2,000 individuals; long uneven lines or large disorderly V with some birds out of formation or gliding; much less organized formation than geese, which do not glide

Migration: complete migrator, to southern states, the Gulf coast, Mexico and Central America

adult | juvenile | drying

Nesting: platform, in a dead tree, usually with branches hanging over the water; male and female build with sticks and driftwood gathered from the immediate area and line the nest with finer plant material and green leaves; 1 brood

Eggs/Incubation: 3-4 bluish white eggs; female and male incubate 25-29 days

Fledging: 37-42 days; male and female feed young

Stan's Notes: A very common bird in Minnesota where it finds adequate lakes for fishing. The most widespread of all cormorant species in North America. The common name "Double-crested" refers to its two nearly invisible crests. "Cormorant" comes from the Latin words corvus, meaning "crow," and L. marinus, meaning "pertaining to the sea," literally, "Sea Crow."

Appears black from a distance, but can have a green sheen when seen nearby. Breeding adults have tufts of black feathers behind the eyes that look like eyebrows, but these are often hard to see.

The cobalt blue color of the eyes are well suited for seeing above and below the water's surface. Can remain submerged for up to several minutes. Catches fish by swimming underwater, holding its wings at its sides. Lacks the oil gland that keeps feathers from becoming waterlogged. To dry off it will strike an erect pose with wings outstretched, facing the sun.

Young hatch up to a day apart (asynchronously) and are fed a regurgitant dripped from the bill of the parent into the chick's open mouth. Young are brooded for up to 14 days after hatching. Parents aggressively defend their nest site, eggs and young from predators. Nests in colonies and usually roosts in large groups in trees close to the water.

Much controversy surrounds this bird because it feeds on the fish that some think should be caught and eaten by people.

American White Pelican
Pelecanus erythrorhynchos

MIGRATION
SUMMER

Size: L 62" (158 cm); WS 9' (2.7 m); WT 15-17 lb. (6.8-7.7 kg)

Male: Large white bird with black wing tips and black along the trailing edges of wings. Oversized bright orange bill with a prominent knob on top, and matching bright orange legs and feet. May have a pale yellow crown. Chick-feeding adult (Jun-Aug) has a grayish black crown. Non-breeding (Sep-Feb) has a bright yellow bill, legs and feet.

Female: same as male

Juvenile: duller white than adult, with a brownish head and neck

Food: fish, amphibians, crawfish

Habitat: large lakes

Sounds: usually silent; gives low grunts and croaks at the nesting site

Compare: The extremely large bill of the American White Pelican makes it hard to confuse with other birds. The Trumpeter Swan (pg. 187) is slightly smaller and lacks the black wing tips and oversized bill. White morph Snow Goose (pg. 167) shares the black wing tips, but is much smaller and has a much smaller, pinkish bill. Western Grebe (pg. 207) and Clark's Grebe (pg. 211) are also much smaller, with shorter, much thinner bills.

Check for colonies of American White Pelicans nesting on islands of large lakes. Look for the oversized orange bill and orange legs and feet to identify.

Flight: glides on outstretched wings, interspersed with strong, deep wing beats; both sexes have a white underside, black wing tips, distinctive black trailing edges and extremely large bill; head is drawn back to shoulders, base of lower bill rests on chest and feet tuck against the tail during longer flights

flight pattern

Flock: 10-200 individuals; large V formation, often gliding, then all flapping together; will circle around repeatedly in a cluster, riding rising columns of warm air (thermalling)

Migration: complete migrator, to coastal Florida, Texas, other Gulf coast states and Mexico

knob on bill

chick-feeding adult

pair

Nesting: ground, on small islands; female and male scrape out a depression and rim it with dirt; 1 brood

Eggs/Incubation: 1-3 white eggs; male and female incubate 29-36 days

Fledging: 60-70 days; female and male feed young

Stan's Notes: One of the largest water birds in North America and becoming much more common in Minnesota. Often seen in big groups during migration on our larger lakes.

Nesting colonies are scattered throughout the state, usually on small islands in big lakes. American White Pelicans share islands with Double-crested Cormorants (pg. 247) and Ring-billed Gulls (not shown). Nesting islands can be loud, active places, with adult birds and chicks milling about, giving their grunting calls.

The bill and legs of breeding adults turn deep orange, and a flat fibrous plate usually grows in the middle of the upper mandible. This plate drops off after eggs have hatched.

Young stay in the nest for 18-24 days and are fed by both parents. The first flight is taken at 9-10 weeks of age. When old enough, young pelicans of various ages band together in large pods and walk around the island.

American White Pelicans don't dive into water to catch fish, like coastal Brown Pelicans (not shown). Instead, many individuals will swim in a line or circle and simultaneously dip their bills in the water to scoop up corralled fish. After netting their meal, they slowly raise their bills, allowing the trapped water–up to 3 gallons (11.4 L)–to drain out the sides. Once the water is drained, the fish are swallowed whole in one or two big gulps.

INDEX

ABOUT THE AUTHOR

Stan Tekiela is a naturalist, author and wildlife photographer with a Bachelor of Science degree in Natural History from the University of Minnesota. He has been a professional naturalist for more than 20 years and is a member of the Minnesota Naturalist Association, Minnesota Ornithologist Union, Outdoor Writers Association of America, North American Nature Photography Association and Canon Professional Services. Stan actively studies and photographs birds throughout the U.S. He has received various national and regional awards for outdoor education and writing. A columnist and radio personality, his syndicated column appears in over 20 cities and he can be heard on a number of radio stations. Stan lives in Victoria, Minnesota, with wife Katherine and daughter Abigail. He can be contacted via his web page at www.naturesmart.com.

Stan authors many field guides for Minnesota including other guides for birds, mammals, reptiles and amphibians, wildflowers and trees, and audio CDs, calendars and notecards.